MUD

OFF-ROAD DISCOVERIES WITH RICH AGUILERA

Pacific Press®
Publishing Association

Nampa, Idaho | Oshawa, Ontario, Canada
www.pacificpress.com

Cover and inside design by Kristin Hansen-Mellish
Cover design resources from the author and thinkstock.com
Interior images are from the author and thinkstock.com unless otherwise noted.

Copyright © 2017 by Pacific Press® Publishing Association
Published by Pacific Press® Publishing Association
Printed in the United States of America
All rights reserved

The author assumes full responsibility for the accuracy of all facts and quotations as cited in this book.

Scripture quotations are from the HOLY BIBLE, NEW INTERNATIONAL VERSION®. Copyright © 1973, 1978, 1984, 2011 by Biblica, Inc.® Used by permission. All rights reserved worldwide.

You can obtain additional copies of this book by calling toll-free 1-800-765-6955 or by visiting http://www.adventistbookcenter.com.

ISBN 978-0-8163-6252-3

February 2017

This book is dedicated to my wife, IVETTE, and my sons, LEO and ALEX, who have been supportive of my ministry work over the years. I would also like to dedicate this book to my parents, RONALD and ZENAIDA AGUILERA, who provided the ultimate example of godly parents and role models on earth.

ACKNOWLEDGEMENTS

I'm grateful to God for giving me the passion and desire to work with young people of all ages. I would like to especially thank RANDY FISHELL for giving me my first opportunity to write about God's amazing nature in *Guide* magazine back in 2008. Randy was the editor of *Guide* when we first met in a chow line at a convention in Tampa. Our conversation continued over lunch as we discovered our mutual passion for young people and cemented a friendship of trust and support.

PREFACE

One of the best ways to get to know our Creator is to study and appreciate His artwork—*nature*. We often get caught up with the busyness of life, but everywhere we go we're surrounded by evidence of God's wonderful, complex design that can be seen all around us in the plants, creatures, and environment we live in.

When we learn about nature we get a deeper understanding of how much God loves us through the way He created this planet to sustain life for us. We often see a tree and think it's pretty, but we sometimes forget that God intentionally designed trees as part of His wonderful master plan to create air for us to breathe and food for us to eat. Every part of nature has a unique place in this world.

I often wonder why things like mosquitoes were created, but then I'm reminded that when the enemy tempted us to disobey God in Eden sin entered the world and all of God's perfect nature became corrupted—including mosquitoes. The good news is that someday Jesus will return to take us home, and He has promised to re-create nature, returning it to His original perfect design. What a day that will be!

In the meantime we should look upon nature with fascination because someday we'll be able to do a "before and after" comparison and be even more amazed by God's original perfect designs!

EDIBLE BUGS

You're probably thinking that the words *edible* and *bugs* don't even belong in the same phrase. Did you know that bugs are loaded with protein? Yum-yum. Could I interest you in a peanut-butter-and-locust sandwich? How about sprinkling a few fried crickets on your haystack?

Bug eating is common just about everywhere in the world except in North America and Europe. The Bible does tell us that some bugs are unclean, though. Check out Leviticus 11:20–23, if you really want to know what God said was edible. Then if you are ever stranded in the middle of nowhere with nothing to eat except some crunchy Bible-approved bugs, feel free to feast! Please pass the chocolate-covered grasshoppers . . .

THE STRONGEST CREATURE ON EARTH!

Pound for pound, the rhinoceros beetle is the strongest creature in the world. It can carry one hundred times its own weight! Let's put that into perspective: If you weigh eighty pounds, it would be like you carrying eight thousand pounds! Imagine yourself carrying a fully grown, four-ton hippopotamus around! This is one mighty bug. By the way, they're totally harmless. Those scary-looking "horns" are used to forage through the jungle floor.

PET SKUNK, ANYONE?

Got a pet at home? A dog, a cat—maybe a bird or some fish? Ever thought of having a pet skunk?

Crazy as it seems, some people keep skunks as pets! Of course, the skunks have been "disarmed" by having their scent glands surgically removed. It seems like a lot of effort just to have a pet skunk, but owners enjoy the animal's curious, playful, and loving nature. There's even an organization of skunk pet owners called "Owners of Pet Skunks" or OOPS.

It's illegal in many places to have a skunk as a pet, so if you or your friends don't have one, you'll have to settle for learning about them from a safe, stink-free distance. (And if you are now hounding your parents to get you a skunk, and they are upset that this particular item appeared in this *Mud* book, tell them to write to the editors, not me. Ha!)

Stinky statistics
- Skunks can spray with amazing accuracy and at distances up to fifteen feet.
- A skunk's scent can carry up to a mile downwind.
- Skunks' bodies contain enough stinky stuff for about five or six sprays. (Let's hope you're the seventh victim in line.)
- It takes about ten days for the scent chemicals to replenish in a skunk's body.

BIZARRE ANIMALS

I'm pretty sure you've been to the zoo many times before and seen all the cute, familiar animals you expect to see in a zoo. If I could build a Mud zoo, here are some of the bizarre animals you'd find there! (Have fun pronouncing their names.)

TARSIER: Tarsiers are small mammals that live in the South Pacific. They're tiny and only grow to about four inches long. Their tail, though, is almost three times as long as their bodies. In proportion to their head, their eyes are huge. They can also rotate their head 180 degrees, allowing them to look and leap backward with precision. No rearview mirror necessary.

GHARIAL: The gharial is related to the crocodile (as I'm sure you can tell from the picture). The most notable difference is the long, pointy snout, which conveniently houses about 110 sharp teeth you don't want to be near. Gharials come from India, but unfortunately in 2007 they were "upgraded" to critically endangered status. They are currently struggling to make a comeback.

SPHYNX CAT: Hey, look, it's a bald cat! Not really. These hairless cats may not have hair, but they do have a fuzzy coat comparable to peach fuzz. When it's cold, the peach fuzz doesn't help much, so they're always trying to find a nice warm place to hang out. Even without hair, their skin still shows distinct colors and patterns that make each one unique.

AXOLOTL: The axolotl is an amphibian unlike anything you've ever seen before. When you get a cut, your body makes new cells to repair the damage. Axolotls have a healing ability that goes one step further. If one of their legs is cut off, they can grow an entire new leg! Because of this unique ability, scientists all over the world study them. Who needs a hospital?

BIZARRE BUGS

If you get creeped out by bugs, you're going to love these specimens. These are some of the most unusual creepy-crawlies in the world. For some reason, even I was feeling itchy while writing this! Still, God made these bugs, and, lucky for you, you don't have to worry about them crawling off the page.

MACRODONTIA CERVICORNIS

After looking at the picture below, you don't need me to tell you that this is a big bug. It can grow up to eight inches long. That's about the height of this page! What's amazing is that even though they're so big, these giant beetles can still fly. Can you imagine riding your bike down the street and running into one of these? Keep your mouth closed and definitely wear a helmet.

PHASMATODEA

These bugs are commonly called "stick bugs" or "walking sticks," and it's pretty obvious why. If you spend most of your time in trees and bushes looking for a leafy snack, what better way to blend in than to look like a stick? Some grow so big you might call them "branch bugs"! The largest ones can be more than twenty-one inches long with their legs stretched out. That's about the length of your arm!

CICADA

The cicada is one loud bug. If this bug were in school, it would be in the principal's office all day for being too noisy. At close range, the "song" of the cicada has been measured at up to 100 decibels. Just think—a lawn mower is about 90 decibels and a car horn is about 110! Unlike grasshoppers, which make noise by rubbing their legs together, cicadas have a vibrating membrane called a timbal that makes all that noise. They can be heard up to a mile away!

GIANT MILLIPEDE

The giant millipede is one of the longest bugs in the world, reaching close to twelve inches in length! Surprisingly, baby millipedes eat the dung of their parents. Yes, that sounds gross, but this makes the food easier for the baby to swallow and also transfers some helpful bacteria from the parent to the baby. Do not try this at home.

EXTREME NATURE!

Meet the **BULLET ANT**, known for having the most painful sting of any insect in the world. People say the pain from a sting is equal to the pain of getting shot with a bullet! The locals call them *hormigas veinticuatro*, which means "twenty-four hour ants," because if you're stung you'll suffer from excruciating pain for one full day.

They're native to Central and South America, so if you don't live there, you're safe.

RICH ANSWERS YOUR QUESTIONS
(WHETHER YOU ASKED THEM OR NOT)

EARTHWORMS

Q: Why do earthworms come to the surface when it rains?

A: Earthworms have no lungs or gills. They breathe through their skin. When it rains and the ground becomes saturated with water, they can't breathe, so they must either surface or drown. (By the way, they don't have eyes or ears either!)

Q: If an earthworm is cut in half, will each half grow into a complete worm?

A: If the back half of an earthworm is amputated, that portion will die, but the remaining front portion can survive, grow a new tail end, and move on with life.

Q: Do earthworms have more than one heart?

A: Yes. Earthworms have five hearts that help pump their blood up and down the length of their bodies. Earthworms can be up to eleven feet long—a long way to push blood!

HOW DO THEY DO THAT?
LIGHTING UP THE NIGHT

On a warm summer night, it's fun to watch fireflies flying around outside. They're a kind of beetle that produces light. That's pretty wild if you think about it, since they don't have any batteries!

Special little organs called photophores on the underside of their abdomen make the light. The firefly's light-producing cells have nerves, air tubes, and two types of chemicals: luciferin and luciferase. When these chemicals combine with oxygen from the air tubes, the reaction produces a greenish-yellow to reddish-orange light.

Not only are these little beetles cool, their light is cool too. Unlike natural and human-made light, their light gives off no heat. This complex process is called bioluminescence, which means "living light."

This reminds me of another Living Light, Jesus! "I am the light of the world," He said. "Whoever follows me will never walk in darkness, but will have the light of life" (John 8:12). Hey, that means you can glow too!

TOP 5 FIREFLY FACTS

Since most people look forward to the sunny days of summer, let's take a look at a summer insect—fireflies.

5. Fireflies are not flies. They're actually members of the beetle family.

4. They are very efficient makers of light. Whereas an incandescent lightbulb uses just 10 percent of its energy to make light, fireflies use almost 100 percent of their light-making chemical reaction.

3. Fireflies taste disgusting. OK—so I've never tasted one. But scientists say their blood contains something called lucibufagins, which taste really gross.

2. The colors of fireflies' light vary. They don't make every single color out there, but different species can produce different colors of light, such as yellow, light-red, green, and orange!

1. Some species can synchronize their flashing. Seriously. It's like synchronized swimming, but fireflies do it with light!

WHAT'S BUGGING YOU?

Is it a bug or an insect? Wait—aren't bugs and insects the same thing? Nope. They're actually different.

When I was a kid, I thought that bugs were the greatest thing around, but it wasn't until I got a little older that I discovered not all insects are bugs. Here are some ways you can tell them apart.

First, it's a fact that bugs are insects, but insects are not necessarily bugs. I know that's confusing, but basically, bugs are simply a type of insect. The main difference is that a true bug has a *stylet*. This means that its mouth is shaped like a straw. A bug uses its stylet to poke and suck plant juices from plants. Some bugs use their stylet to suck blood from other creatures, but let's move on. . . .

Another way of knowing if an insect is a true bug is by its wings. A bug's front wings are harder and thicker than a wannabe bug. The wings are also colored near where they attach to the bug's body. Sometimes the wings act like a little roof covering the entire back of the bug's body. Finally, the bug's hind wings are usually clear and tucked under their front wings.

So is a ladybug really a bug? No, it's an insect. The reason is because its mouth has pincers and it chews its food. Because of this, scientists often refer to them as something else: ladybirds, or ladybird beetles.

The next time someone asks you, "Hey, what's bugging you?" you'll know if it's an insect or a real bug that's bugging you!

THE DISGUSTING COCKROACH

I like to collect fossils. Here is a picture of one of my favorites: it's a small chunk of amber with a cockroach that got stuck inside. If you've seen me doing "LIVE! (and Muddy)" at your church recently, then you've gotten a close-up look at this same fossil.

You don't need me to tell you that cockroaches are pretty gross, so I'll just give you a few interesting facts about these creepy-crawlies and let you enjoy that squirmy feeling.

A COCKROACH CAN
- live for almost a month without food;
- live for about two weeks without water;
- live for up to one week without its head (That's gross!);
- hold its breath for up to forty minutes; and
- run up to three miles per hour. (That's fast for a tiny bug!)

BIZARRE BIRDS

It's time for some more bizarre nature! We're going to look at bizarre birds. When most people think of birds, they think of nice colorful parrots or high-flying eagles or cute little sparrows. Well these bizarre birds are about as far from a typical bird as you can get. Check out these strange feathered friends.

First, there is the **helmeted hornbill**, which comes from the rain forests of Malaysia and Indonesia. The most obviously bizarre feature on this bird is its bill. What makes it unique is that this bird's bill is not hollow—it's solid and very heavy! The bill makes up 10 percent of the bird's weight. It must have strong neck muscles!

This is a **king vulture**, and it sure has some unusual things happening on its head that make it "handsomely ugly." These birds are expert gliders and can quietly glide for hours without flapping their wings as they look for lunch. These birds do not have a voice box. The only noises they can make are a few croaking and wheezing sounds.

Wikimedia Commons

Our next specimen is one strange-looking bird. It's called a **shoebill**. It's hard to tell from the picture, but this is a very large bird that grows to about five feet tall. (That's about as tall as many of you readers out there!) Can you imagine walking through the jungles of Africa and coming face-to-face with one of these birds? Hello... gotta go.

This blue beauty with the cool-looking hairdo is a **Victoria crowned pigeon**, named after Queen Victoria. (How would you like to have a bird named after you?) These are the largest pigeons in the world; they stand about as tall as a turkey!

BIZARRE SEA LIFE

Ah, yes, it's time for more stranger-than-fiction natural life-forms. Do you know why I enjoy the weird stuff so much? It shows how everything God made is unique. Here are some really different creatures God put in the oceans.

YETI CRAB

Although it looks like this crab needs a haircut, those aren't really hairs. They're more like bristles. Scientists discovered this creature just six years ago, and there's still a lot they don't know about it.

LEAFY SEA DRAGON

What better way to hide from your predators than disguising yourself as seaweed? The leafy sea dragon lives only in the waters off Australia and grows to about fourteen inches long. The female lays up to 250 eggs at a time. She turns the eggs over to the male, who carries them around for four to six weeks until they hatch. (In football that's called a handoff.)

VIPERFISH

This is one of the most creepy-looking fish lurking in the deep seas. Its teeth are so big they don't even fit in its mouth! Its lower jaw is hinged in a way that will allow its mouth to open especially wide. Viperfish grow to about twelve inches in length, but with teeth like that I wouldn't want to be on the receiving end of their bite.

BLUEBELL TUNICATES

They look more like a plant, but they're animals. They lay eggs, which become larva. The larva swim around until they're big enough to find a nice spot to park themselves permanently. Once they find a spot, they do something very unusual—they digest their cerebral ganglion. That's the equivalent of eating your brain. Do not try this at home.

NO MAP NECESSARY

Not long ago a *Guide* reader, "Chipmunk," asked why homing pigeons don't get lost.

Homing pigeons have an amazing ability to find their way back home. The pigeons are raised at point A. Then they are transported in a box or cage to another location. When the pigeons are released, they fly back to point A. In some cases, they are able to return home over extremely long distances—up to one thousand miles away. That's incredible!

Our question writer, Chipmunk, lives in Florida. If she were to take a homing pigeon to New York and release it, the pigeon could return home all by itself!

You may have seen pigeons released at a wedding or on a TV show. Those are homing pigeons. They don't just take off and fly away—they return to their home.

So how can they find their way without getting lost? Uh, I don't know. Actually, no one really knows (except the One who created them)!

Scientists have been trying to figure out why pigeons don't get lost. Here are some of their ideas:

- Pigeons may be able to sense earth's magnetic field and use it to orient themselves.
- They may use olfactory navigation—sniffing their way home.
- As a pigeon nears home, it may recognize landmarks it has seen before.

Maybe you'll be the one who finally figures it out!

NATURE'S WORLD RECORDS

When I was a kid, my favorite book was *The Guinness Book of World Records*. Some of the stuff in there was pretty strange, but it always had a lot of interesting facts. Well, let's take a look at some of nature's world records!

FASTEST BIRD:
Peregrine falcon (dives at speeds of more than two hundred miles per hour)

FASTEST INSECT:
Dragonfly (can move at thirty-six miles per hour)

LONGEST WORM:
Bootlace worm (can be more than 180 feet long)

LARGEST BAT:
Giant fox bat (wingspan of more than six feet)

LONGEST-FLYING BIRD:
Sooty tern (can go three to ten years flying and floating without touching land)

INSECT WITH SHORTEST ADULT LIFE SPAN:
Mayfly (lives as little as one hour)

FASTEST-GROWING PLANT:
Bamboo (can grow at a rate of three feet per day)

LONGEST SEA CREATURE:
Lion's mane jellyfish (largest found was seven feet wide with tentacles of more than 120 feet long)

CUTE KILLERS

Don't be fooled by looks. Some animals look sweet and innocent, but they may be deadly! Take, for example, the moose. Don't be fooled by that goofy grin. Moose attack more people than bears do. Moose don't like to be bothered, and when they feel threatened they charge, as in "Get out of here or you're toast!" Here are a few other "cute killers" you should be aware of.

Slow loris

Aw, isn't she cute? The slow loris is one of the only poisonous mammals in the world. Its poison is located next to its elbows. One of the ways it protects itself and its young is by spreading some of the poison on its body in case something is tempted to bite it. When threatened, the loris takes some poison into its mouth, mixes it with saliva, and bites. (If I made poison, the *last* place I would think of putting it would be in my mouth!)

Golden poison frog

This cute little frog is considered by many to be the most poisonous vertebrate in the world. Its skin is drenched in alkaloid poison, which can cause a person's heart to stop. The poison on the frog's skin makes them taste terrible to all predators. This frog's poison can kill an animal or human who simply touches it.

VENOMOUS OR POISONOUS?
WHAT IS THE DIFFERENCE?

VENOM is a toxin that a creature injects into its prey or enemy. The creature usually does this by biting or stinging. Some examples of venomous creatures are rattlesnakes, bees, and scorpions.

POISON is a toxin that a creature doesn't have to inject because the creature's entire body or parts of its body are poisonous. Some examples of poisonous creatures are frogs, toads, and the slow loris.

Just remember:
- Venom is often used to catch lunch.
- Poison is helpful so you don't become lunch!

BIZARRE RELATIONSHIPS

It's time for another look at some bizarre things around us. This time we're looking at bizarre relationships. No, I'm not talking about you and your siblings. I'm talking about relationships between things in nature. Check 'em out!

Ants and aphids

Aphids consume sap from plants, but then they excrete a sweet substance called honeydew from their body. The ants like the honeydew. Yum.

When a plant no longer provides sap for the aphids, ants will carry the aphids to new plants. When it starts getting colder, aphids lay eggs. Ants carry the eggs to their own underground nursery and care for them until spring. When it's warm and the eggs have hatched, the ants take the baby aphids out and put them on healthy plants. All this so the ants can enjoy some sweet honeydew.

Blue sea slug and Portuguese man-of-war

OK, I really don't know who's coming up with these names, but we're basically talking about a type of nudibranch (sea slug) and a venomous marine animal that is similar to a jellyfish. Blue sea slugs feed on the Portuguese man-of-war and can eat the whole thing—poison and all. The sea slug is able to isolate and store the poison for its own defensive use.

Imagine you're borrowing someone else's poison so you can protect yourself. And what do you do? You go and swallow it! If you think about it, this system had to be designed to work perfectly from the start. I mean, how could sea slugs ever *evolve* into something able to swallow poison?

Elephant ear plant and scarab beetle

The elephant ear plant relies on the scarab beetle for pollination. Elephant ear plants grow a flower stalk with three types of flowers: male, female, and sterile. The three look exactly the same. The beetles love to eat the flowers, but they eat only the sterile flowers. While the beetles chomp on the sterile flowers, they move the pollen between the male and female flowers. The amazing thing is that the male and female flowers are never eaten, so the plant can grow! This plant grows a third type of flower that it sacrifices in order to get the beetles to come and pollinate the flowers.

Monarch butterfly and milkweed

Birds like to snack on butterflies and moths, but they avoid the monarch butterfly. As a caterpillar the monarch eats only

from the milkweed plant, which is poisonous to many animals. The monarch caterpillar, however, can eat the milkweed and simply store the poison in its body its whole life, even after it turns into a butterfly. The monarch's bright colors are a warning to hungry predators: Nasty snack—avoid.

WACKY ANIMAL TRIVIA!

Since I write about nature, it's pretty obvious that I love animals. Sometimes I'm asked questions on the *Guide* about animals. Here is some unusual animal trivia you may not have heard about.

- In Alaska it is legal to shoot bears. However, waking a sleeping bear for the purpose of taking a photograph is prohibited.
- The catfish has more than twenty-seven thousand taste buds—the most of any animal.
- Fish that live more than eight hundred meters below the ocean surface don't have eyes.
- It is possible to lead a cow upstairs but not downstairs.
- Snails can sleep for three years without eating.
- Crocodiles swallow stones to help aid in digestion and to help them control buoyancy in water.
- Koalas are excellent swimmers.
- Bats always turn left when exiting a cave.
- Slugs have four noses.
- Snakes have just one lung.
- A group of crows is called a murder.

WEIRD OCEAN CREATURES

There are some really strange creatures in the ocean. At least to humans they seem strange! *(I suppose they think we look pretty strange too.)*

One such strange creature is the pyrosome. Pyrosomes are small marine creatures that measure just a few millimeters in size and have a saclike body. What's interesting is that they often live in large colonies.

Pyrosomes are bioluminescent, which means they can create their own light. Some pyrosome colonies are so large that their blue-green light can be seen from one hundred feet away!

God has filled our planet with amazing creatures. Thanks, God, for being so, well, creative!

ELEPHANTS—I LOVE 'EM!

If you ever ask me what my favorite animal is, you will always get the same answer—elephants!

A few years ago I was able to travel to Africa. I got to spend a week on a safari, and I took these pictures of elephants. One of the most impressive things to see is a herd of forty to fifty elephants in the wild. The oldest female in the herd is the boss. She is called the matriarch.

One day I was driving in South Africa when I came across a herd of elephants crossing the road. Fascinated, I didn't realize I had gotten too close to the herd. Immediately, the matriarch started to charge my car, flapping her ears and trumpeting loudly. Yikes! I backed away from there as quickly as I could!

RICH ANSWERS YOUR QUESTIONS
(WHETHER YOU ASKED THEM OR NOT)

We all have questions, but we don't always get answers. So right here, right now, I'm going to provide you with answers, even if you didn't ask the questions. You're welcome. The topic is **ELEPHANTS**, the largest land animals alive today.

Q: How do I tell the difference between African and Asian elephants?

A: The most noticeable difference is their ears. African elephants' ears are more than twice as large as Asian elephants' ears. (Those big ears are great for fanning their owners in the hot African savanna.)

Q: How important is the elephant's trunk?

A: The trunk is an elephant's most prominent feature. Elephants use their trunks to drink, eat, pick up things, and spray water and dirt on themselves to cool off. While a human's entire body has less than one thousand muscles, an elephant's trunk alone has about one hundred thousand muscles!

Q: Do elephants have fingers?

A: Elephants don't have fingers similar to the ones humans have, but on the end of an elephant's trunk it has grabbers called fingers that allow it to pick up small objects. African elephants have two fingers on the ends of their trunks, but Asian elephants have only one finger.

SPEEDY ANIMALS

It's a rough world out there. After the entrance of sin, animals began hunting each other for food. This means that being a speedy animal comes in very handy! This Mud Top Ten looks at the world's fastest land animals. *Zoom!*

10. Coyote. Top speed: forty-three miles per hour. Coyotes are good jumpers. (They can cover more than thirteen feet in a single leap.)

9. Elk. Top speed: forty five miles per hour. Given their weighty antlers, it's amazing they can run so fast and still keep their balance!

8. Cape hunting dog. Top speed: forty-five miles per hour. This is the fastest dog in the world. Greyhounds top out at about thirty-nine miles per hour.

7. Quarter horse. Top speed: 47.5 miles per hour. The horse is the fastest domesticated animal in the world. Giddyup!

6. Springbok. Top speed: fifty miles per hour. These animals can jump more than eleven feet vertically and fifty feet horizontally in a single bound! "Springbok" is definitely a good name for them!

5. Wildebeest. Top speed: fifty miles per hour. They are known to listen to the alarm call of other animals when a predator is around. Time to get moving!

4. Thomson's gazelle. Top speed: fifty miles per hour. Their major predators are cheetahs, which are faster, but Thomson's gazelles can outlast cheetahs in long chases. They can also make turns more abruptly.

3. Lion. Top speed: fifty miles per hour. Since lions can run fast only in short bursts, they try to sneak up on their prey. When they are within one hundred feet or so, they will attack.

1. Cheetah. Top speed: seventy miles per hour. Cheetahs can go from zero to sixty miles per hour in about three seconds. Enough said.

2. Pronghorn antelope. Top speed: sixty-one miles per hour. This is the fastest animal in North America. Pronghorns have a very large heart and lungs to help them sustain high speeds.

THE VENUS FLYTRAP

The Venus flytrap is a unique plant because it eats bugs. The plant captures its meal using a pair of lobes that can close to trap insects when they are walking in the trap. Their bait is a sweet mucilage—a sticky liquid that attracts insects.

Inside the trap there are six tiny trigger hairs. When two of the hairs are touched within a twenty-second time period, the lobes quickly close and trap their lunch inside. If their catch gets away, the lobes open up again within twelve hours.

Once it has successfully trapped a snack, the Venus flytrap starts to digest the insect by releasing enzymes around the bug to break it down. About ten days later the lobes open up again. All that is left is the empty husk of the insect. The plant is now ready to catch the next insect that steps into its trap.

MIGHTY SHRIMP

One of the most unusual sea creatures is the mantis shrimp. It is a marine crustacean, distantly related to lobsters and crabs. It's called a mantis shrimp because it resembles both a shrimp and a praying mantis.

The interesting thing about this creature is how incredibly strong its claws are. Some species of mantis shrimp have clublike claws that they use to smash their meals apart. The claw is very handy when they are craving something inside a shell, such as a clam.

The mantis shrimp strikes by rapidly unfolding and swinging its claws at an acceleration as fast as that of a bullet. *Bam! Gulp.* If the first strike misses, the resulting shock wave can sometimes be enough to stun or kill the prey too!

Even if their prey is much larger, with their little claws the shrimp can inflict serious damage. On rare occasions they have even been known to shatter standard aquarium glass. *Let me outta here!*

BIZARRE DEFENSE MECHANISMS

The Bible says that when humans first sinned, God's punishment was a curse that affected men, women, serpents, plants, and all of nature. This could explain why many creatures have defense mechanisms to help them survive in a sinful world. We all know that skunks spray and opossums play dead, but let's check out some of the most bizarre defense mechanisms in the world.

HORNED LIZARD

The horned lizard's prickly appearance certainly helps to protect it, but looking scary is not a bizarre enough defense for this creature. No, it has a much more startling approach. When attacked, it creates pressure in its sinus cavities until small blood vessels in its eyes burst and spray blood on its attacker. The blood can spurt as far as five feet! Apparently, the blood tastes very nasty to many predators. I'll take their word for it.

HAGFISH

Hagfish grow to about eighteen inches long. When captured and held, the hagfish oozes out an incredible amount of nasty slime that expands into sticky goo. The slime suffocates its predators by clogging up their gills. How does the hagfish get out of that sticky mess? It ties itself into an overhand knot and moves the knot from head to tail, scraping itself free of its own slime!

SEA CUCUMBER

The sea cucumber has a fascinating defense mechanism. If it is being threatened and needs to escape through a small crack, it can absorb water through its skin, "goopify" its body into mush, and then slip through a tiny opening. Once it's safe, it can go back to a solid state so nothing can drag it out of its hiding place. That's why they call it bizarre!

BOMBARDIER BEETLE

If you bother this little bug, it will spray you with a pulsating jet of foul-smelling, chemically toxic boiling fluid that explodes in your face. Nice, huh? You can even hear the explosion of the hot vapors that shoot out at five hundred to one thousand pulses per second!

Wikimedia Commons

INCREDIBLE ANIMALS
THESE FROGS ARE CHILLIN'!

When it gets cold and starts snowing, I get out my coat, gloves, and hat. Wood frogs have another way of dealing with the cold—they freeze solid! As the temperature drops they burrow themselves under some leaves or a log, and their liver starts pumping out glucose through the bloodstream to all the organs. Glucose is like antifreeze, protecting the organs from damage. When the glucose has been pumped everywhere, they stop breathing, their heart stops pumping, and most of their body freezes solid! They can stay like that for months while they wait for winter to pass. When spring comes and the temperature warms up, they begin to thaw. First their heart starts pumping again. Then they start gulping air. Soon they're happily on their way to find the nearest pond. God thinks of everything! (Kids, do *not* try this at home!)

ANIMAL BABY NAMES!

OK, everyone, it's time to test your knowledge on animal baby names. Everyone knows a baby dog is called a puppy and baby cats are called kittens. Those are a piece of cake, but not all animals are that easy. Try to match up the animal name to its baby name! You can find the answers on page 128.

porcupine	spat
turtle	gosling
cockroach	puggle
goose	joey
turkey	kit
ant	calf
oyster	cub
cheetah	owlet
ferret	peachick
swan	maggot
platypus	kid
kangaroo	antling
goat	larva
camel	cygnet
peacock	poult
owl	nymph
fly	hatchling
bee	porcupette

BIZARRE BEHAVIOR!

It's time for another round of bizarre nature. Sure, this stuff is pretty strange, but it shows us how creative God is, and I love creativity! We're going to look at some bizarre animal behavior seen on our planet. Check out these four specimens:

Tree-climbing goats

The Tamri goats of Morocco have a very special ability: They can climb trees! What drives them to this odd behavior? The delicious fruits and leaves of the argan trees. They must be pretty tasty to drive a goat to go out on a limb.

Upside-down goldfish

Once in a while goldfish do something very odd: They swim upside down. Goldfish owners say it looks like they're playing dead, but experts say the fish just ate too much or swallowed too much air with their food. This can affect the swim bladder, which helps the fish stay balanced.

Cows with compasses

Thanks to images from Google Earth, scientists looked at photos of eight thousand cattle from around the world and discovered that when grazing or resting, cows tend to face either magnetic north or south. Who needs a GPS?

Cuckoo parents

These birds don't like parenting. They lay their eggs in the nests of other birds and leave to do their own thing. The new host bird keeps the eggs warm, and when they hatch, the adoptive parents still feed and care for the babies! No wonder they call them cuckoo.

TOP 5 MARINE CREATURES

The ocean is an amazingly big place, and we've barely started to understand its vastness. Let's take a look at a few fascinating facts about the life God created in the oceans.

Sea horse

The sea horse does something that no other species does—the male gives birth to the young! The female puts up to fifteen hundred eggs into the male's small pouch, much like a kangaroo. There the eggs grow until the male releases them. Thanks, Dad!

Glass squid

This creature grows to be from four inches to ten feet long! This animal is called the glass squid because it is transparent. Playing hide-and-seek as a kid must have been interesting!

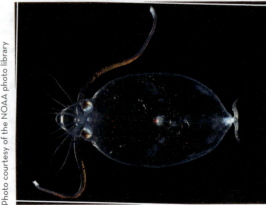

Photo courtesy of the NOAA photo library

Sea sponge

Sponges have no head, no mouth, no eyes, no heart, no bones, no lungs—not even a brain. Yet they are living animals! Their bodies are full of pores and channels that allow water to circulate through them so they can get food.

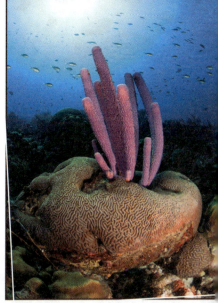

Dolphin

These guys are the kings and queens of cute. Everyone loves dolphins! Did you know that when one dolphin is sick or injured, other dolphins come to help it by bringing it to the surface to breathe? That's very cool!

Crab

Crabs are decapods, which means they have ten legs. Also instead of having teeth in their mouths, they have teeth in their stomachs!

TOP 5 CUTEST CREATURES

If you've been reading my column in *Guide* for a while now, you know I often feature some pretty strange and bizarre creatures. I want to try something different. I'd like to mention some of the cutest creatures out there. Yes, this is the softer side of Rich. Enjoy it while you can—sometime I may write about a disturbing and disgusting bacteria growing in your mouth.

CUTIE NO. 5 MEERKAT

When it's time to forage for food, meerkats take turns standing as "lookouts" while the rest of the community eats.

CUTIE NO. 4 PENGUIN

Even though it's a bird, it spends about half of its life in the water.

CUTIE NO. 3 CLOWNFISH
Come on, can a fish get any cuter than this? Did you know that there are no clownfish in the Atlantic Ocean?

CUTIE NO. 2 RED PANDA
Even though the name says panda, it's not a bear. It's actually related to a raccoon and a skunk.

CUTIE NO. 1 HARP SEAL
Do I really need to say anything about this cutie?

YUCKY PARASITES!

As you know, besides writing this column once a month in *Guide*, I also answer the questions you post on the *Guide* Web site. If you've never visited the Web site, you should!

Recently, one of you asked me to write about tapeworms and other gross things. It sounds like its time for more yucky stuff!

Tapeworms are flatworms that live in the intestines of some animals that have become infected while grazing or drinking contaminated water. If you're wondering if a human can get tapeworms, the answer is yes. The main cause of tapeworm infections in humans, though, is not from grazing. (That would be a curious sight, though.) For humans, tapeworms are the result of eating the meat of infected animals. Here's a picture of what tapeworms look like. (Yeah, yuck!)

If you're wondering what's involved in removing tapeworms from people, there are several medicines that can help get them out. I'm sure it's not a fun process though.

These creatures are also known as parasites. Parasites are creatures that survive off another creature, called a host. The parasite benefits from being there, but the host usually doesn't even know the parasite is living there and that it's hurting the host. (That's not very nice—bad parasite!) One of the most common parasites in people is this nasty intestinal invader called giardia.

If you ask me, the best word to describe a parasite is *lazy*.

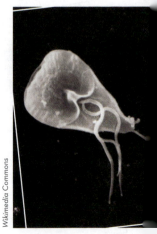
Wikimedia Commons

The Bible says a lot about lazy people. It says that they are foolish, that they will end up having crummy jobs, and that they will not fulfill God's purposes. When you grow up, be a hard worker and help care for those who can't care for themselves! So don't be a parasite.

Clearly, no one wants to have something inside of them that can harm them. Sound familiar? Check this out: Satan is a parasite. He wants to live inside of you, and his only goal is to hurt you. The medicine for getting Satan out of your body and mind is to ask God to help you be pure and clean. You have to do your part and be careful what you allow in your body. I'm not talking about raw meat; I'm talking about the movies and TV shows you watch, the books you read, and the video games you play. If you aren't careful, allowing bad things into your mind will allow Satan to plant parasites in it that will hurt you. I pray that you will always be protective of what you allow into your mind.

On this page are some pictures of other types of parasites. Some are pretty hurtful, some are pretty common—others are just plain disgusting!

CHECK OUT THESE VERSES:
Proverbs 12:24; Proverbs 10:4; Matthew 25:26.

GREAT GROSSIES

Part of my job for *Guide* is to gross out everyone once in a while. It sure is fun to look at some of the strange things found in nature. Here are a few classics you need to know about. Get ready; some of these will make your skin crawl—literally!

EYELASH MITE
You guessed it—they live on your eyelashes and other body hair. I know, that's creepy, but don't worry; they're pretty harmless. They live only about two weeks. I'm not sure if that's good or bad.

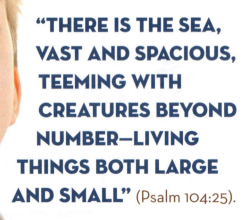

"THERE IS THE SEA, VAST AND SPACIOUS, TEEMING WITH CREATURES BEYOND NUMBER—LIVING THINGS BOTH LARGE AND SMALL" (Psalm 104:25).

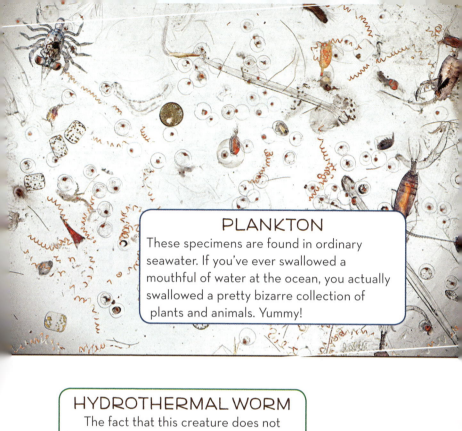

PLANKTON
These specimens are found in ordinary seawater. If you've ever swallowed a mouthful of water at the ocean, you actually swallowed a pretty bizarre collection of plants and animals. Yummy!

HYDROTHERMAL WORM
The fact that this creature does not live on our bodies makes me feel better about it. These are deep-sea creatures that live at the bottom of the ocean. This one sure looks hungry.

COOKIE MONSTER OF THE SEA?

Some of you may have grown up watching Cookie Monster on PBS, but the last place you would expect to see him is in the ocean. After all, he'd get soggy!

Not long ago some divers in the Caribbean came across a purple sea sponge that looked a lot like mister "me want cookies." Apparently, the divers concluded that three separate tube sponges had fused together this way.

Here are some other cute and funny animals!

How did you know I was collecting nuts?

Help! Someone please bring me honey!

How could you not be afraid of heights

MARINE CREATURES

The ocean is an incredible place. Most people don't appreciate just how much life exists in the oceans. There are such mammals as whales and otters. There are also such reptiles as turtles and sea snakes. Such birds as penguins and albatrosses also live in marine environments.

Of course, a huge portion of the life-forms in the sea are fish and invertebrates. Invertebrates are creatures that do not have a backbone, such as clams, jellyfish, and octopus. (Don't forget the corals too!)

That's not all. There's hugely diverse plant life in the ocean

Photo Courtesy of Uwe Kils

too. From seaweed to algae, these plants play an important role in providing food for ocean creatures.

Finally, there are microscopic life-forms that live in the ocean—inhabitants such as phytoplankton and zooplankton. These are the tiniest creatures in the ocean, so small that you need a microscope to get a good look at them! This is a picture of a type of plankton called a tomopteris.

If God took the time to carefully design and create even the tiniest creatures of the ocean, imagine how much He loves His most prized creation: you!

WHAT ABOUT THE DINOSAURS?

I get asked about dinosaurs once in a while. Well, I wish I knew exactly what happened to them. As I've read and researched about dinosaurs, here are a few conclusions I've drawn from my personal studies.

Scientists have found entire skeletons, teeth, droppings, tracks, eggs, and even soft tissue from dinosaurs. My first conclusion is that dinosaurs really existed.

In Genesis 1:25, the Bible says: "God made the wild animals according to their kinds, the livestock according to their kinds, and all the creatures that move along the ground according to their kinds. And God saw that it was good."

The second conclusion I draw is that God created all the creatures of the earth. Satan does not have the power to create. He may have the power to corrupt, but only God can create. So I believe God created dinos.

My third conclusion is that eventually these animals became extinct. I believe that most of the animals on the planet perished

Artist's conception of Triceratops

at the time of Noah's flood. Genesis 7:15 says: "Pairs of all creatures that have the breath of life in them came to Noah and entered the ark." Were a few types of dinosaurs saved on the ark? After all, dinosaurs were "breathing" animals. If so, they may have become extinct sometime after the Flood.

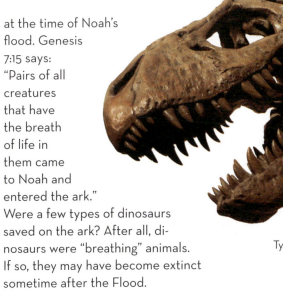

Tyrannosaurus Rex

My fourth conclusion is that dinosaurs obviously got to be pretty large animals. The Bible says that before the flood people lived a very long time. "Altogether, Methuselah lived 969 years, and then he died" (Genesis 5:27). Is it possible that animals also lived longer than they now live? A two hundred-year-old cow? A fifteen-hundred-year-old turtle? A six hundred-year-old lizard? Did you know that reptiles are the only kind of animals that never stop growing throughout their lives? All dinosaurs are classified as reptiles. I wonder what would happen if a lizard continued growing for six hundred years?

I can't wait to get to heaven so I can ask Jesus exactly what happened to all those large animals!

Komodo Dragon

TOUGH QUESTIONS:
WHY WERE DINOSAURS SO BIG?

I liked dinosaurs when I was a kid. The funny thing is that as an adult, I still think they're pretty fascinating! Of course, there's a lot we don't know about dinosaurs, but let's try to tackle this question: Why were dinosaurs so big?

Here's a possible explanation. If you read through Genesis 5, you can see that the first generations of people on earth lived more than nine hundred years. But after the Flood something changed. Within a few generations a human's typical life span was shortened to under one hundred years. No one knows exactly what happened, but something changed.

So here's an important question: If humans could live more than nine hundred years, don't you think it's possible that animals lived longer lives too? Maybe a horse could live for four hundred years? Maybe an elephant could live for six hundred years? Maybe a reptile could live for five hundred years? Seems like a possibility. Since it is thought that reptiles never stop growing and that most dinosaurs were reptiles, then if a reptile could live for five hundred years and never stop growing, it seems as though it would grow to be pretty large. That is one possible explanation.

WOOLLY MAMMOTHS: WHEN DID THEY LIVE?

Every once in a while on the news you'll hear about another frozen mammoth found in a place such as Siberia or Alaska. As you can imagine, the report usually says that these big, furry elephant relatives lived tens of thousands of years ago.

The Bible teaches that a global Flood rearranged the surface of the earth about 4,350 years ago. Did woolly mammoths live after the Flood? It appears that they did. Here are a few reasons why:

1. Mammoths are often found near rivers, tar pits, caves, rock shelters, sinkholes, and peat bogs. These are natural features that many experts believe could have been formed only after the Flood.

2. Mammoths are often found in glacial till—that's the leftover sediment from a retreating glacier. This suggests that the glaciers were formed after the Flood.

3. Drawings of mammoths are found in caves. This indicates they lived alongside humans.

4. Most of the mammoth bones found have not been fossilized. Minerals have not replaced the organic matter, and some even still have bone marrow!

The Bible is a book of truths. It shows us God's authority and power. Sometimes people try to replace God's authority with their own explanations. Trust the Bible to get your truths, and you'll see that nature and science confirm the things of the Bible!

BACK FROM EXTINCTION!

Once in a while I read in the news about creatures that have become extinct recently. This makes me sad. One of the most famous examples is the dodo bird, which has been extinct for several hundred years now. It was native to the island of Mauritius in the Indian Ocean. Unfortunately, dodoes couldn't fly, nor were they afraid of humans so many were killed off. In addition to that, humans also destroyed their habitat and food source. If that wasn't enough, humans accelerated their extinction by introducing pigs, dogs, and other predators to the isolated island. Way to go, humans.

But once in a while I hear about a species that was thought to be extinct, but has been rediscovered in a remote corner of the world. Recently, near the famed ruins of Machu Picchu in Peru, a group of researchers discovered a cat-sized chinchilla that was thought to be extinct for hundreds of years. The full name of the comeback creature is the Machu Picchu arboreal chinchilla rat. Way to go! Now that it's back, maybe we can come up with a cuter name for it.

THE OTHER EXTINCTION

Did you know there is a second classification of "extinction" called "extinction in the wild"?

It means that a certain creature is extinct in their natural habitat, but living versions exist in captivity. For example, there is a popular fish called the *Ameca splendens* that is thought to be extinct in the wild but survives in captivity in fish tanks all over the world. It's awesome that it lives on, but if you think about it, the ultimate purpose is for a creature to function within its natural habitat. If they exist only in captivity, they are already ecologically extinct.

When I think about extinction, it always reminds me of a verse in the Bible in which God told humans we would have dominion over the creatures of the earth. I'm pretty sure this didn't include killing them all off. I hope we continue to see more creatures making a comeback!

Here are two more neat animals that are extinct in the wild.

SCIMITAR ORYX
Extinct in the wild since 1998

GUAM RAIL
Extinct in the wild since the 1980s

Wikimedia Commons/Greg Hume

In my blog I have posted a link for a video of the twenty-five most endangered species on earth. Check it out! **www.GuideMagaine.org/mud**

TWO COOL ANIMALS

God made some pretty amazing creatures. Check out these two interesting specimens.

SEA OTTERS

Sea otters love the water so much that they eat in it, give birth to their pups in it, and they even sleep in it! They lay belly-up in the water and catch their nightly zzzs. Sometimes they hold the paw of another otter so they don't float away alone.

MIMIC OCTOPUS

The mimic octopus is one of the most unique creatures in the world. Many animals use mimicry (looking like another animal) as a survival strategy, but the mimic octopus appears to be able to copy the appearance of several different species, not just one. What makes it even more amazing is that all the species it imitates are venomous!

POLAR BEARS

Below are some interesting facts about polar bears.

- Polar bears have black skin under their fur.
- A polar bear's entire body has fur, even under the paws!
- Polar bear fur looks white, but it's actually transparent.
- Polar bears are among the world's biggest bears. Males can be more than eleven feet long!
- Only pregnant female polar bears hibernate.
- Polar bears are born blind and deaf. Human babies are pretty helpless too. Our parents have to do everything for us. In a spiritual sense, we are blind; we don't understand God. As we get older and learn what God has done for us, we "see," and make a decision to follow Jesus. When we do that, our spiritual blindness goes away, and we can see how wonderful it is to be one of God's children. By the way, it doesn't end there. Once our blindness is gone, God wants us to help others see Him too!

CREEPY CRAWLIES

Do you like insects, tolerate them, or simply think they're creepy? Some people like insects. After reading these unusual bug facts, perhaps you'll fit into a new category!

Plenty for all!

When you're out in the country, does it feel as though there are billions of insects around you? Maybe that's because there are more insects in one square mile of rural land than there are humans on the entire planet! Have you ever gotten a cut that required stitches? Can you imagine your skin being held together by ants? When army surgery ants are placed on a cut, the creature bites the edges with its mandibles, sealing the wound for days. Once the ant is attached, its mandibles stay on the cut. (I'll take my stitches the regular way, thank you.)

Regular hornets are quite terrifying, but the Asian giant

ACTUAL SIZE

hornet is one you will definitely want to avoid. The photo on the previous page shows how big they can grow. Second, their stinger is a quarter of an inch long and can inject a large amount of venom, enough to kill a human (even if they are not allergic) if stung several times. Third, they're intense predators. Because of their large mandibles, a single hornet can kill as many as forty honeybees per minute by quickly decapitating them when the hornet attacks the bees' hive. Fourth, they're really fast. They can fly up to twenty-five miles per hour and travel up to sixty miles in a day! Finally, they have the ability to apply a scent to their target in order to invite the rest of the colony to know where to attack a food source. Quite the friendly insect.

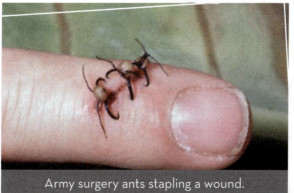
Army surgery ants stapling a wound.

UNFAVORITE ANIMALS

On the *Guide* Web site, many of you have requested facts about animals. Keep reading, and keep giving me ideas for things you'd like to read and learn about!

When most people are asked about their favorite animals, the list usually includes many of the same creatures. I feel bad for some animals that are probably never selected as favorites. That's why I'm writing about "unfavorite animals." I've picked a few that probably never get picked as anyone's favorite.

Ticks

The ghastly tick might just be everyone's least-favorite creature. These parasites live off the blood of mammals, birds, and other creatures. They also carry lots of diseases.

Aye-ayes

Not every animal has been blessed with good looks. Aye-ayes live only in Madagascar and are the only known primates to use echolocation to find food. They tap on trees with their finger and listen for yummy wood-boring insects under the bark to eat.

Scorpions

Surprisingly, scorpions are related to ticks. Some species have poison strong enough to kill a person. Maybe that's why I've never heard anyone say that scorpions were their favorite creature.

Giant anteaters

These toothless animals are famous for poking the ground with their long tongues, which they use to help them eat about thirty-five thousand ants and termites per day. Those tongues can reach two feet out of their mouth!

In a sinful world I don't know if God has an unfavorite animal, but I'm sure that He has no unfavorite human beings. He loves each one of us so much that His Son, Jesus, chose to give His life to save us. Clearly, we are God's favorites!

SNAKES

OK, let's keep things really simple. Here is my list of top five snakes you really don't want to mess around with. You'll see why.

Black mamba

This is one of those super-ultra venomous snakes. It's very aggressive, and one bite can make a human collapse within forty-five minutes. Without treatment a person can die from this snake's bite. If you see one of these, I have one simple piece of advice: *Run!* They are found in Africa, so unless you're in Africa reading this, don't worry about the black mamba for now.

Rattlesnake

The rattlesnake is usually found in North America, so you might want to pay a little more attention now. If you live in Africa, you don't have to worry about this one too much. You need to keep worrying about the black mamba. Fortunately, when the rattlesnake senses danger, its tail creates a rattling noise. Thanks for the warning!

Philippine cobra

I put this one on my list because not only are they venomous, but they can actually spit their venom at their prey. These snakes can usually be found in the northern parts of the Philippines, and they like to hang around in the water. They prey on rodents and frogs. The venom causes respiratory failure—in other words, the prey can't breathe!

Tiger snake

You don't see too many animal names that are made up of two different animals, but this is one of them. This snake has a very venomous bite, and a person can die in as little as thirty minutes of being bitten. What makes this guy extra-creepy is that it can grow to be about seven feet long! It is usually found in Australia and Tasmania.

Belcher's sea snake

Yes, snakes can swim too. This one can be found in northern Australia and southeast Asia, and this sea snake bites when provoked. Its bite's symptoms can appear between thirty minutes to several hours after the bite. Some scientists believe its venom is one of the most potent and concentrated venoms out there.

In the beginning, when God created the world and everything in it, everything was perfect. There wasn't even death. The Bible tells us that because of sin, all things in nature became severely affected. Before sin there was no venom or poisonous plants, no thorns or cancer or pain. I can't wait till Jesus returns, because when He does, we will be taken to heaven, where we will be re-created as God had originally created us—perfect!

WHAT'S THE DIFFERENCE?

When God designed and created all the creatures of the world, He displayed incredible variety, but in some creatures there are obvious similarities. Can you tell frogs and toads apart? How about dolphins and porpoises? Have no fear: this table is here to help you sort out these important things!

TURTLE & TORTOISE

HABITAT—Turtles live aquatic lives; tortoises live on land.
FEET—Turtles have flippers or webbed feet; tortoises have short, sturdy feet.
SHELL—Turtles have flat, streamlined shells; tortoises' shells are heavy and dome-shaped.

ALLIGATOR & CROCODILE

SNOUT—Crocodiles have a long, narrow v-shaped snout; alligators have a wider u-shaped snout.
SIZE—Crocodiles are larger than alligators.
TEETH—When their mouth is closed, crocodiles' teeth are very visible; alligators' teeth are harder to see.

DOLPHIN & PORPOISE

FIN—Dolphins' dorsal fins are tall and curve back; porpoises' are triangular.
SIZE—Dolphins are longer and leaner than porpoises.
BEAK—Dolphins have a pointed beak; porpoises have a shorter, rounder nose.

RABBIT & HARE

SIZE—Hares are bigger and faster than rabbits.
EARS—Hares have longer ears and hind legs than those of rabbits.
COMMUNITY—Hares are solitary; rabbits live in groups.

SEALS & SEA LIONS

EARS—Sea lions have visible ear flaps; seals don't.
FLIPPERS—Sea lions' front flippers are longer than seals'.
SWIMMING—Seals are better swimmers; sea lions get around easier on land than seals do.

FROGS VERSUS TOADS

Frogs and toads are both amphibians, but what's the difference between them? For a lot of people this is confusing, since they look so similar. Maybe we should also ask, What is an amphibian? Let's get to the bottom of this!

The word *amphibian* means "creature that lives a double life," because these animals start off with gills and tails in the water, then eventually grow lungs and legs and live on land. As for the difference between frogs and toads, here's a little chart:

FEATURE	TRUE FROG	TRUE TOAD
Skin	Smooth and moist	Bumpy and dry
Teeth	Teeth in upper jaw	No teeth
Eyes	Eyes bulge out from body.	Eyes don't bulge out from body.
Hind legs	Long jumping legs	Shorter hopping/walking legs

Frogs and toads go through big changes as they grow into adults. Right now you are also going through some changes as you grow into an adult. Some of the changes can be hard and odd, but I hope you will stay close to God. He will help you as you turn into an adult. Remember, you are already a wonder of God's artistry!

MAKE YOUR OWN FROG

If you are looking for a great Sabbath afternoon activity, try building this **paper frog**! Go to the Mud page at **www.guide magazine.org** to print the free pattern. With scissors, glue, and some patience, you'll soon have a three-dimensional frog.

Want another paper challenge? Make an origami frog out of a U.S. dollar! Watch the video instructions at the *Guide* Web site.

Instead of drinking water, frogs soak it into their body through their skin. They also absorb half of the air they need through their skin.

Frogs can see forward, sideways, and upward all at the same time.

A group of frogs is called an army. A group of toads is called a knot.

A frog's sticky tongue is attached to the front of its mouth, not the back.

TOP 5 ODD CREATURES

Here are some animals that you've probably never seen at a zoo or farm or anywhere else. Check 'em out.

5. RED-LIPPED BATFISH
They have nice lips, but they're terrible swimmers. Most of the time they walk along the bottom of the ocean. They are found near the Galapagos Islands.

4. UMBONIA SPINOSA
This is a type of thorn bug. It pierces a plant stem with its beak and feeds on the sap. They're not considered friends of farmers, so maybe the cool handle on top makes them easy to grab. Just sayin' . . .

3. SAIGA ANTELOPE

Their unusual nose makes them unique. (By the way, each of you is unique, too, and I hope that you never make fun of someone else because they're a little different.)

2. INDIAN PURPLE FROG

These purple, small-headed, and pointy-snouted frogs spend most of their life underground. They come to the surface only about two weeks per year—to mate. Their favorite snack is termites. Hungry yet?

1.

And my number 1 animal that you probably didn't know existed is the SEA PIG, not to be confused with the sea cow, or manatee. Sea pigs live on deep ocean bottoms, and they get their food by extracting organic particles from deep-sea mud. I guess that's where the "pig" part comes from—land pigs like to hang out in the mud too!

SMART BIRDS!

Parrots are considered by many to be one of the most intelligent species of birds in the world. Most people know that they have an amazing ability to imitate the talking sounds that a human makes, but many people don't know that they are also skilled at using tools and solving puzzles. They are smart birds!

Imitating human words is a pretty neat skill, but it reminds me about how Satan is trying to put many bad role models in our world for us to imitate too. It might be an actress, a singer, or even a sports figure who behaves badly. Be careful whom you imitate, whose example you follow. We need to be smart and choose to imitate only Jesus! He is the ultimate role model!

Ephesians 5:1, 2 reads, "Follow God's example, therefore, as dearly loved children and walk in the way of love, just as Christ loved us and gave himself up for us as a fragrant offering and sacrifice to God."

LIONS ON SAFARI!

A few years ago I went to Africa on a safari with my wife for a couple of weeks. Of course, I didn't take a weapon, but I did have my camera with me! My goal was to see if I could spot all of the "big five" animals: elephant, Cape buffalo, leopard, rhinoceros, and lion. I didn't get to spot all five, but at least I saw four of them. The only one I didn't get to see was the elusive leopard.

Of the five, the one I was most looking forward to seeing was the lion, the "king of the jungle"! We got to see lions a few times, including a lioness with five cubs! Here are a few cool lion facts I learned while in Africa:

- When a lion roars its loudest, it can be heard up to five miles away! They would not do well in libraries.
- Lions are the only feline species in which the males and females look noticeably different.
- Lions are the only big cats that live in social groups, called prides.
- Lions sleep up to twenty hours a day. They don't sleep in—they just rest all the time!
- Only lions have a tuft of dark hairs on the tips of their tails, which some people think helps them communicate.

"I'M READY FOR MY NEXT NAP."

THE DOGGY DILEMMA

A couple hundred years ago there were only a few varieties of dogs. Today some kennels recognize up to about four hundred different dog varieties. Most scientists agree that all these dogs originally came from some sort of wolf-dog parent animal. What has happened to dogs during the past two hundred years?

In the 1800s it became very fashionable to own dogs, so people started sorting and classifying dogs with certain characteristics and breeding them in order to have more of that same variety. If they wanted to enhance certain features of a dog, they would selectively breed dogs that had those features.

Unfortunately, this selective breeding by humans has caused major problems with the dog kind. Forcing certain traits to become prominent in dogs, we've actually created bigger problems with many dog breeds.

Purebred dogs are the ones with the biggest problems. Keep in mind that pure breeds are forcibly created by breeding two dogs from a limited gene pool. When that happens, the risk of inheriting genetic defects grows dramatically.

I've included a few images that show how dramatically some dog varieties have changed in the past one hundred years.

The German shepherd is considered by many to be a ruined breed. It often has a barrel chest, sloping back, and several other problems. A few of these dogs can jump over a seven-foot wall, but many are not able to because of genetic-related problems.

Pugs have also changed a lot. Besides the shorter legs and stocky

body, they have difficulty breathing and suffer from high blood pressure, heart problems, teeth problems, and skinfold problems.

Now many of these "purebred" dogs are susceptible to a variety of problems and diseases. Let me give you one of the most dramatic examples—the bulldog.

Back in the mid-1800s the bulldog looked more like today's pitbull—sturdy and athletic with a longer muzzle. By the early 1900s it had become a popular breed, and bulldogs were bred to have squat legs, a larger head, and a flattened muzzle. After

one hundred years, bulldogs suffer from breathing problems, malformation of their hip joints, skin and heart problems, and several other defects. They also have one of the shortest life spans in the dog world. To make matters worse, all these changes have made it almost impossible for them to mate naturally, and when the females give birth, the puppy's head has become so big that it doesn't fit through the birth canal, and puppies need to be removed surgically! Not only did human intervention create this breed in the first place, but

many scientists agree that the bulldog breed would be extinct now without additional human intervention.

What's the point? Messing with God's nature seems to make things worse. Living things are

already affected by sin, so when humans think they are so smart that they can mess with biology, they often make matters worse. God created science, so let's make sure we use science in a responsible way that gives glory back to the Creator!

BIZARRE TREES

Did you know there are about one hundred thousand different species of trees in the world? That's a lot of creativity! But I think God was feeling extra-creative when He came up with these bizarre trees. Check them out.

Banyan tree
I'm sure you've seen it before—the tree roots are in the ground and then comes the trunk, and then the branches are on top, right? Typical tree. The thing is, the banyan tree is not very typical! The branches of the banyan tree send down dangling roots that eventually reach the ground to make more roots in the ground. Eventually, this becomes one sturdy tree!

Dragon tree
You want to know how old a tree is? You could cut it down and count the rings. But that's pretty drastic! Besides, that technique wouldn't work on the Canary Islands dragon tree. Because it's not really a tree—just a very large plant—there are no rings! Instead, people estimate the dragon tree's age by counting how many times the branches have forked and how many times it has flowered. (Doesn't seem very accurate to me.)

Redwood tree

Coast redwoods are the tallest trees in the world. Some of these trees grow taller than the length of a football field! Redwoods grow only in a few spots along the Pacific coast of the United States. I sure hope the birds that nest up there aren't afraid of heights.

Baobab tree

This has to be one of the strangest trees out there. People say it looks like it's upside down and the roots are sticking up in the air! Well, that chubby trunk stores enough water for nine dry months in the African savanna. (Maybe they should've called it the camel tree.) During those nine months the baobab tree doesn't have leaves; it's just hanging out, surviving till the rains come again.

SUPERVOLCANOES VERSUS EVOLUTIONISTS

A supervolcano is an extra-large volcano that can produce devastation on an enormous, even continental scale—a catastrophic event.

Evolutionary scientists argue that it took millions and billions of years to form the various landscapes we see on this planet.

But the effects of a regular volcanic eruption, such as that of Mount St. Helens in 1980, show that such huge time spans aren't necessary. In just a few years, this single "small" catastrophic event formed thick layers of rock and fossils and created huge canyons that supposedly should have taken millions of years to form.

Just another evidence that a catastrophic event—such as a worldwide flood—can do the same amount of damage as "millions" of years of erosion.

Do *you* live near an active volcano? Go to the Mud section at **www.guidemagazine.org** and click on the "Volcano Map" link to find out!

Check out Mud online at **www.guidemagazine.org** to see an on-location video about the volcanoes in Hawaii. See what happens when I poke lava with a stick!

VOLCANO CHECKUP

Is that volcano alive? A volcano's health status generally falls into one of three categories:

1. **Extinct:** Dead volcanoes. They're not coming back.
2. **Dormant:** Volcanoes that are taking a quiet nap. Watch out, though—they might wake up one of these days.
3. **Active:** Volcanoes that still rumble and toss out lava. There are about 1,550 active volcanoes on earth.

NIGHT LIGHTS

An unusual phenomenon occurs in the sky near the north magnetic pole. It's called the aurora borealis or northern lights. A similar phenomenon happens at the south pole.

These light shows are caused by the **solar wind**. The sun is so hot that its outermost gases blow away as solar wind, made up of charged particles that take two to five days to reach earth.

When particles from the solar wind blow to earth, they interact with one of the upper layers of our atmosphere, called the magnetosphere. The atoms and molecules become energized and glow. The aurora borealis looks like a glowing curtain of light hanging in space.

EXTRA! The best time to see the aurora borealis is from August to April.

EXTRA! The aurora borealis has been seen as far south as Florida.

EXTRA! The bottom edge of the aurora's glowing curtain of light is about sixty to seventy miles above the surface of the earth.

BIZARRE LAKES

I have already talked about some of the most bizarre **trees** in the world, now I want to tell you about some of the most bizarre **lakes** in the world! Check them out.

Boiling Lake

There's a small island in the Caribbean Sea named Dominica that is home to a strange lake with a name that says it all—Boiling Lake. This is one lake you do *not* want to take a swim in because the temperature around the edges has been measured at almost two hundred degrees Fahrenheit. It's really a flooded fumarole, basically a hole in the earth where steam and volcanic gases escape. The volcanic heat causes the water in the lake to constantly boil. This lake is **hot, hot, hot!**

Crater Lake

Crater Lake in Oregon is the deepest lake in the United States, almost two thousand feet deep, and it sits on top of a mountain in an ancient crater. The interesting thing about this lake is that it's called one of the cleanest lakes in the world. There are no inlets or outlets to this lake, so all the water comes from rain and snow. The average snowfall at Crater Lake is forty-four feet per year! Glad I don't have to shovel snow up there.

Lake Baikal

This lake in Siberia is unique because even though on the

surface it's smaller than Lake Superior, it's what's below that counts. About 20 percent of the world's fresh water is in this *one* lake. In fact, Lake Baikal holds more water than all five of the Great Lakes in North America combined. Why? Because it's almost a mile deep! If you accidentally drop something in this lake, forget you ever had it.

Dead Sea

What a creepy name. Why do they call it the Dead Sea? Pretty simple—nothing lives in it! There is so much salt in the water that no plant or animal can survive. How salty is it? Take a gallon of water and put *two* pounds of salt in it. If you stand at the shore of the Dead Sea you will be standing at the lowest dry spot on earth, over a thousand feet below sea level. The salty water is very dense, so almost

everything floats in it like a cork—including *me*!

THE UPS AND DOWNS OF TIDES

Have you ever wondered why there is a low tide and a high tide? We know winds and currents move the water on the ocean's surface, but what makes the surface elevation vary so much? The highest variation is in the Bay of Fundy in Nova Scotia, Canada. There can be almost a forty-five-foot variation from low to high tide!

A high tide is a bulge of water created by the gravity of the moon (as well as the sun sometimes). Just as the gravity of our earth causes things to fall toward the ground, the moon also has gravity that causes the oceans to swell up when the moon is directly above. As the earth turns and the moon changes position, the swelling moves around the earth, causing the height of the oceans to rise and fall.

Since the water on the planet is spread out evenly, when the oceans facing the moon experience high tide, so does the opposite side of the earth. In the meantime, the "sides" of the earth experience low tide. When the moon, earth, and sun are all aligned, it causes maximum tides such as the 44.6-foot variation in the Bay of Fundy.

When the tide went out, this boat was left stranded.

WATER AND WINTER

When winter is upon us, for many of us that means snow! I love snow. Each winter I look forward to sledding, snowboarding, skiing, skating, and building snowmen. I even enjoy removing the snow from my driveway! None of these activities would be possible if it were not for the unique properties of water.

Water is the only natural substance found in all three states—solid, gas, and liquid—at normal earth temperatures. When you boil water, it turns into steam. When you freeze water, it turns into ice.

If you are at sea level, water will boil at 212 degrees Fahrenheit. But did you know that if you were on a mountain fourteen thousand feet above sea level, water would boil at 186 degrees Fahrenheit?

Ice is fascinating too. When you freeze water into ice, it becomes lighter than water. That's why ice always floats. Pretty cool . . . I mean, pretty cold!

Water is amazing. Without water nothing on this planet could live. Speaking in spiritual terms, that's why Jesus said, "Whoever drinks the water I give him will never thirst. Indeed, the water I give him will become in him a spring of water welling up to eternal life" (John 4:14).

Check out Mud online at **guidemagazine.org** to see a video about snow. Watch out for snowballs!

CLOUDS 101

Are all clouds the same? Nope. Here is a crash course on nephology, the study of clouds.

There are three main types of clouds: cirrus, cumulus, and stratus. Different combinations of these three types of clouds make up the ten or so varieties we see in the skies.

Cirrus clouds
These are those wispy-looking clouds in the sky. They are actually the highest clouds, usually floating more than nine miles high. It's pretty cold up there, so the water in these clouds freezes to form ice crystals. When you see cirrus clouds, it usually means there will be a change in the weather within twenty-four hours.

Cumulus clouds
Who put those big ol' fluffy balls of cotton in the sky? Those are cumulus clouds. Just because a cloud is a cloud, that doesn't mean it's going to rain. When you see cumulus clouds, it actually means the weather will be dry!

Stratus clouds
These clouds often seem endless. They usually form a uniform gray cloud that covers the entire sky. If you can't see any blue, you're probably looking at a stratus cloud. These are some of the lowest clouds in the sky, about one mile above the ground.

CLOUD IN A BOTTLE

Since we're talking about clouds, here's an experiment you can try that allows you to make your very own cloud. (I tested this at home, and it *does* work. Pretty cool, actually.)

Stuff you'll need:
- two-liter clear plastic soda bottle
- matches
- very warm water

Making a cloud requires a couple of ingredients. First, fill about one third of the bottle with very warm water and put the cap on. As the warm water evaporates, vapor collects inside the bottle. Vapor is water in the form of a gas. Vapor is our first ingredient.

Next, you'll need the match. Make sure you have permission to use it! Remove the cap, light the match, and drop it into the bottle. Put the cap on quickly, trapping the smoke inside. Smoke, dust, and other particles floating around in the air form our second ingredient.

Our third ingredient is a drop in air pressure. Slowly squeeze the bottle hard. A cloud will appear when you release pressure, and it will reappear when you squeeze the bottle again. You made your very own cloud!

In the Bible, God often manifested Himself in a cloud. Remember the cloud the Israelites followed for forty years? Also, at His second coming, Jesus will return in a cloud!

RICH ANSWERS YOUR QUESTIONS (WHETHER YOU ASKED THEM OR NOT)

CORAL

Q: Is coral an animal or a plant?

A: Coral looks like a plant but is really an animal. One of the main differences between plants and animals is that plants make their own food, while animals have to consume food.

Q: So, how do corals eat?

A: The parts that look like flowers or branches are actually tentacles that capture food from the water. Corals have a mouth too. It's a tough way to get a meal, since they have to wait for their lunch to float by!

Q: How much coral is there in the world?

A: Coral reefs cover less than 1 percent of the ocean floor, but they are home to 25 percent of all fish species on the planet.

DID YOU KNOW?

- Twenty-five percent of coral reefs have already disappeared.
- Coral reef organisms are an important source of new medicines.
- Coral reefs are in crisis and are dying all over the world.
- Coral reefs protect the coasts from hurricanes and tsunamis.
- At the current rate of destruction, about 70 percent of the world's corals will be destroyed by 2050.
- A coral grows in one stable spot for its entire life.

Visit **www.guidemagazine.org/mud** to learn how we can help protect coral reefs. There's also a Webcam with a live peek into a reef!

WINTER THUNDERSTORMS

Imagine you're outside building a snowman and suddenly you see a flash of lightning and hear the sound of rolling thunder. There's definitely something wrong with that picture! In reality, though, it is not that uncommon to have thunderstorms and lightning in winter. There are three scenarios in which lightning can be observed during the US winter season:

1. "Normal" thunderstorms. Of course, not everyone in the United States experiences the same winter weather. If you live in the southern half of the country east of the Rockies, the warm air from the Gulf of Mexico allows the conditions needed for severe weather. Occasionally that warm and moist air makes its way north, allowing for a "normal" thunderstorm in the northern states too.

2. Thundersnow. You may never have even heard of this word! It is possible for strong winter snowstorms to produce lightning strikes called thundersnow. They are quite rare because they require unstable and intense conditions.

3. High-elevation lightning. Lightning is common in very high mountain ranges during strong storms any time of year. As you know, when lightning strikes, it usually hits tall objects. If you are on a tall mountain during a lightning storm, there are not many places to hide!

News flashes about lightning
- Satellites can see and calculate that there are about three million lightning flashes around the world each day. That's forty flashes per second!
- A lightning flash is no more than one inch wide.
- Lightning moves about sixty-two thousand miles per second—one-third the speed of light. That means

lightning could circle our planet five times in two seconds. *Speedy!*
- Central Africa has the highest frequency of lightning strikes in the world. In the United States the lightning hot spot is Florida.

Don't get zapped

When lightning strikes, the electrical charge is trying to find the most direct path to the ground. Since trees and buildings and houses are elevated, lightning often hits them first. The question is: where does the electricity go when it hits a house?

Most houses are filled with wires and metal pipes that serve as a perfect path for the electricity to get to the ground. So normally you won't feel the lightning if you're in the house. The problem is that if you are near one of those metal pathways as the electricity is passing through, it can jump to you, and you can get zapped.

Water and electricity don't go well together either, so don't take a bubble bath during a lightning storm, even if you really need a bath. Just tell your folks I gave you permission to stay stinky for a little while longer.

LIGHTNING SAFETY TIPS

During a lightning storm:
- Get into a large enclosed building. Avoid small sheds and open pavilions.
- If you're in a car, roll up the windows and stay inside.
- Stay a few feet away from open windows, sinks, toilets, electrical outlets, and so forth.
- Avoid using a corded phone. (Cordless and cell phones are OK.)

TREASURES OF THE RAIN FOREST

If our planet were a body, the Amazon rain forest would be the lungs, because 20 percent of the planet's oxygen is produced there. Unfortunately, the rain forest is being destroyed at an alarming rate, and many parts of earth's environment are being affected. Some experts believe that

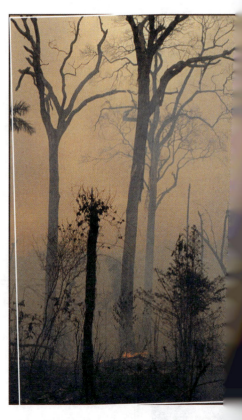

- one and a half acres of rain forest is destroyed every second; almost one hundred acres may be lost in the time it takes you to read this page.
- we are losing 137 plant, animal, and insect species every day because of the deforestation.
- 25 percent of our medicines come from rain forest ingredients, but less than 1 percent of the trees and plants have been tested for medicinal value. And more than half of the world's estimated ten million species of plants, animals, and insects live in tropical rain forests.

Let's do what we can to be good stewards of God's creation.

RICH ANSWERS YOUR QUESTIONS
(WHETHER YOU ASKED THEM OR NOT)

BARNACLES

When I was growing up, I was a curious kid. The moment something grabbed my attention, I had to run to our set of *World Book* encyclopedias and look it up. Of course, in the process I would also end up reading five other totally unrelated articles!

Well I will save you a trip to the encyclopedia by answering the questions you haven't asked about the topic you didn't know you were going to ask me about till just now: barnacles!

Q: Is a barnacle a plant or an animal?

A: A barnacle is a type of arthropod, an animal that has its skeleton on the outside. Barnacles have one eye and twelve feathery limbs that catch plankton for food.

Q: Can barnacles move around?

A: Typical barnacles are sessile feeders. That means they are permanently attached to objects such as a rock or the hull of a ship. Barnacles start out as an egg for several months until they are released by their parents as free-swimming larva, looking for their own place to settle. Once they find a spot, they cement themselves to the surface headfirst for the rest of their lives. (And you thought *your* life was boring.)

Q: Is it true that barnacle shells have doors in them?

A: Yes (sort of). A typical barnacle has six calcified plates that it builds for protection. Two of those plates can be moved across the opening when the barnacle is not feeding. It's like opening and closing a set of doors!

HUMONGOUS FUNGUS

Earth's largest living object is considered to be a giant fungus called *Armillaria ostoyae*, or the honey mushroom. Don't expect to walk into the forest and see a massive mushroom. This fungus primarily grows underground and spreads through a network of rhizomorphs, rootlike structures as seen in the picture below.

Scientists have collected samples of the fungus from a widespread area in Oregon and analyzed its DNA. Test results have shown that it is one single organism estimated to be about twenty-four hundred years old and about the size of fourteen hundred football fields!

WITH A FUNGUS THAT SIZE, THERE ISN'T MUSHROOM FOR ANYTHING ELSE! (GET IT?)

GOOD OLD MOLD

Have you ever stumbled across an apple in your locker at school that had been in there way too long? Chances are that it didn't look like it did on the day it was picked. It was probably covered with mold. Oops.

That's gross, you think, but hold on a second. Is mold such a bad thing?

Like mushrooms, mold is a fungus. It grows on food and other organic matter. Its job is to break things down into slime so it can get the nutrients it needs to grow. Mold is one of nature's cleaners. It is a very important part of nearly every ecosystem in the world because it helps to break down dead organic material and put it back into the soil.

Did you know that food producers use some molds in food? Yes, blue cheese is *supposed* to have mold. Maybe you didn't know that soy sauce is also made with mold!

One of the most important medicines we have—penicillin—is made from mold. Millions of people have been saved by it because it fights disease and infections. Many other lifesaving medicines are made from mold.

Next time you say "yuck" at the sight of mold, think again. God knew exactly what He was doing. Where would we be without good old mold?

Would you like to see how soy sauce is made? Visit **www.guidemagazine.org**.

EXPERIMENT: FREEZING POINT

Perhaps you've probably forgotten about winter. Or maybe you live in a place that doesn't get to freezing even then. Or maybe you're right in the middle of winter as you read this. This experiment involves freezing some stuff.

First let me ask: What is science? One dictionary says it's learning something by observation and experimentation (sort of like the kid in the picture).

How about trying a less-painful science experiment? You should have all of the items around your house that you'll need for this experiment.

- two paper or foam cups
- salt
- water
- freezer

Fill the two cups with the same amount of water. In one cup add four tablespoons of salt and mix it until the salt has dissolved in the water. Mark that cup with a big "S" so you know which one has the salt. The other cup should only contain water.

Put both cups in the freezer. (Make sure they're on something flat so they don't tip over.) Most freezers are kept about zero to

four degrees Fahrenheit, well below freezing, so you will need to keep checking every few hours to see what happens. Check again the following morning. What's the difference between the two cups?

This is a simple example of science. You did an experiment and learned something by observing the results.

Evolutionists claim that we evolved from slime into fish, then frogs, then apes, then people. They say our planet and everything on it have been evolving for billions of years. Evolutionists claim that science proves their theory.

But can a person do a scientific experiment to prove that this is really how things happened? No. Was anyone around to observe evolution happening?

No. Of course, evolutionists believe that their observations of nature support their ideas, but no experiment or observation can prove evolution. In other words, a person must exercise a certain amount of faith to believe in evolution.

It requires faith to believe in creation too. I believe that the physical evidence we see all over our planet points to God as our Creator. I choose to trust the Bible, and I'm glad Bible truth never changes.

THIS PLANT IS OUT OF CONTROL!

Salvinia molesta is an invasive plant. That means it grows so fast that it creates problems for other organisms trying to live around it.

This aggressive aquatic plant is originally from Brazil. It floats on the water and doubles in size every few days. If left unchecked, it will soon completely cover a lake in a thick mat. The picture at the bottom of this page looks like a nice grassy park somewhere, but it's actually a lake that has been completely invaded by *Salvinia molesta*.

The plant prevents sunlight from entering the water, which prevents other plants, and creatures as well, from surviving in the water. Not only that—it's hard to remove. If you leave a little piece behind, it will simply spawn a new plant and continue growing relentlessly.

Lake Kariba in Africa had an encounter with this extreme plant starting in the 1950s. Within three years *Salvinia molesta* had covered two hundred square miles of the lake! That is one speedy plant.

BIZARRE NATURE:
TRAVELING ROCKS

Some time ago I traveled to Death Valley, the hottest, driest, and lowest place in the United States.

One of the more unusual natural features of Death Valley is the bizarre moving rocks. These unique rocks vary in size and mysteriously move across the bottom of a dry lake bed floor, leaving a trail in the dry mud. Some have moved as far as fifteen hundred feet over the years. No one has ever observed them moving.

Most theories about how these rocks travel include rain, which supposedly makes the lake bed into a very slippery, muddy surface. Now add some strong gusts of wind to get the rocks started, plus strong sustained winds to keep them moving. Since no one has actually seen this happen, no one knows for sure if the rain-wind theory is correct, but it sure beats "aliens" as one of the possible explanations!

THE TONGUE

OK, we all have one, and we need it to talk. Here are my top five facts about the tongue.

5. The human tongue has between three thousand and ten thousand taste buds.

4. On average, women have shorter tongues than men.

3. The tongue's taste receptors cannot actually taste food until saliva has moistened it.

2. The blue whale has the largest tongue of all animals. Its tongue weighs almost six thousand pounds! That's more than the weight of an average car!

1. Sticking your tongue out at people is seen as childish or rude in many countries. However, in Tibet it is considered a greeting. (Kids, don't try this at home.)

TONGUES OF FUN

Can you name the five elements of taste perception? I'll give you the first letter of each word.

S__ S__ S__ S__ B__

Can you curl your tongue into a tube at the front?
Can you turn your tongue over?
Can you touch your nose with your tongue?
Try quickly saying RED LEATHER YELLOW LEATHER!

THE ZOO IN YOU

It's a jungle in your mouth! Did you know there are more than five hundred types of living organisms in your mouth? There are more bacteria in your mouth than there are people in the world! If you count every part of your body, there are roughly one trillion bacteria hanging out with you right now.

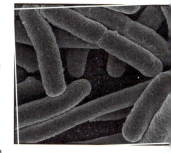

Bacteria are everywhere. They're in the water, in the air, and in every living thing on the planet. Some bacteria are good, some are bad, and others are just *ugly*!

GOOD: The *good* bacteria in our bodies help us digest our food and make medicines and vaccines. They also maintain our immune system and fight off the bad types of bacteria.

BAD: *Bad* bacteria get into our bodies and make us sick with food poisoning, strep throat, and other not-so-fun sicknesses. How do they get into our bodies? One of the main ways bad bacteria spread is through bad hygiene.

UGLY: As for the *ugly* bacteria—there are bunches out there that you don't want to get. E. coli (pronounced ee *coe-lie*) is one that will turn your guts into mush and kill you if you don't treat it. Getting killed by a microscopic bug would not be fun.

What can you do? Learn more about the different bacteria and always wash your hands!

STUPENDOUS CELLS

If you listen to the news once in a while, I'm sure you've heard the term *stem cells* before. But what exactly are stem cells?

You may already know that cells are the tiny building blocks that make up living things. For example, roughly nine months before you were born, you were made up of just one lonely cell. The next day you expanded to two, then four, then eight. Today, your body is made up of at least ten trillion cells! Here's what that number looks like with all the zeros—10,000,000,000,000.

Different types of cells are needed for different body parts. There are certain types of cells for your bones, organs, muscles, and all the other body parts that make you, well, you.

Cells are amazing because if you break a bone or cut your skin, your cells in those areas get to work, repairing and fixing the damage.

A stem cell is a little different. This is a cell that has not yet "figured out" what it will turn into. Scientists are now discovering how to make stem cells grow into the types of cells needed to repair injuries or damaged cells in various parts of the body.

Scientists will try to use this science to do great things to benefit humanity. But in the end, life is an incredible gift that can only come from God.

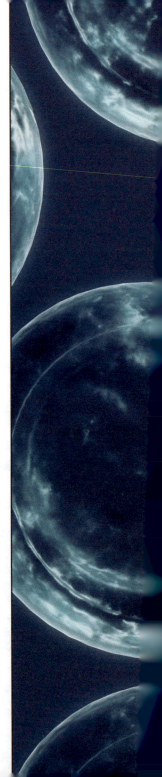

HOW DO THEY DO THAT?
HEALING A WOUND

Being young can be painful. As you can imagine, when I was a kid I wanted to be outside every possible moment of the day. It seems as if I got scraped, cut, and bruised on a daily basis.

Fortunately, God designed and created the human body to do incredible things. One of the most amazing things our bodies can do is repair themselves. It's called *regeneration*.

The three main things found in blood are *platelets*, *red blood cells*, and *white blood cells*. The liquid that carries all that stuff around is called *plasma*.

The main job of the *red blood cells* (pictured below) is to take oxygen and nutrients to every part of your body.

When you get a cut, *platelets* immediately go to the cut. They stick together and try to clog up the opening so blood stops leaking out.

At the site of the cut, germs may get into the body. The job of your *white blood cells* is to immediately go to the cut and start fighting off the bacteria so you don't get an infection.

Regeneration makes our bodies whole again. It reminds me of forgiveness. When people hurt each other with words, the best way to repair the damage is with forgiveness.

NATURE'S LEFTOVERS

Ever heard of vestigial organs before? They're organs that supposedly serve no purpose anymore but can still be found in our bodies. Most evolutionists claim that vestigial organs are "left over" from evolutionary change. The classic example is a little organ you may have heard of called the appendix. It's even possible that some of you reading this have had your appendix removed.

Since scientists can't explain why the appendix is there, many try very hard to fit it into evolutionary theory. Here's one approach: Since (they claim) our ancestors were apes and ate only plants (they say), it's possible that the appendix produced a type of bacteria that would help digest these plant foods. But since (they claim) apes evolved into humans (they suggest), somewhere along the line humans started eating more meat and the appendix slowly lost its usefulness.

Believe it or not, the evolutionists may be right—about the veggies-to-meat diet, that is, not the apes-to-humans part.

Bible believers understand that God originally gave humans plant foods to eat. It was only after sin came along that humans started eating meat, so it's possible that the change in diet and the long-term effects of the curse could be an explanation for our mysterious little appendix. Of course, we don't *know* if that's the reason. When we don't even know for sure what the organ did in the first place, it's hard to guess what it "stopped" doing!

On the other hand, some scientists believe the appendix does have a purpose, and several possible functions of the appendix are currently being explored.

It's cool that scientists out there are curious enough to spend so much time trying to figure out where we came from and how everything came into existence. Let's just keep the Bible as our ultimate source of truth.

EYE TEST

Do you trust your eyes? When you look at the picture above, your eyes tell your brain that all you see is a blob of colors. But there's more! This is a stereogram, and there's a word hidden in this picture. To see it, try these tips: Look at an imaginary object twice as far away while focusing on this image, or hold the page up close to your nose and slowly move it away from your eyes.

Did you see the word? Your own eyes can fool you sometimes.

When Jesus was resurrected, Thomas couldn't believe his eyes. He had to double-check that it was really Jesus. But then Jesus told Thomas, "Blessed are those who have not seen and yet have believed" (John 20:29).

In the end, it's best to believe with your brain, not your eyes.

Check page 128 for the answer.

GOT HALITOSIS?

Halitosis? That's a fancy way of saying bad breath. When it's time for bed, probably Mom or Dad reminds you to brush your teeth first. That's cool—everyone knows cavities are not fun. Still, in the morning you may wake up with bad breath. What happened? Did you sleepwalk to the kitchen and eat an onion during the night?

No. Bad breath occurs for various reasons.

If you don't brush and floss enough, decaying food particles and bacteria will get trapped in your mouth. Remember, your mouth is a warm 98.6 degrees Fahrenheit, so it's an ideal environment for stuff to sit and rot if you don't clean it.

Saliva helps to wash bacteria out of your mouth, but at night saliva production goes down, so stinky bacteria are allowed to stay and play.

Also, when you don't drink enough water, your mouth isn't able to make as much saliva to clean the bacteria out of your mouth.

Of course, if you did eat an onion last night, then you shouldn't be too surprised about having bad breath in the morning.

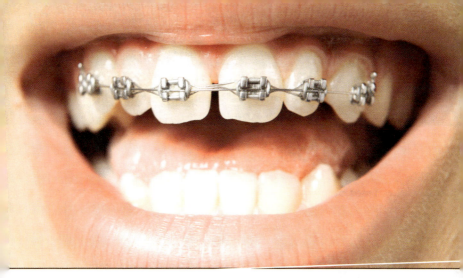

THE TEAM IN YOUR MOUTH

Many of you are in the process of getting your twenty-eight permanent teeth in your mouth right now. You should have them all by the time you're about twelve or thirteen. There's more, though! You also still have another four teeth coming—wisdom teeth—but they won't appear till you're between seventeen and twenty-one years old. They're called wisdom teeth because they come in when you're "old" (and wise, hopefully).

Teeth have all sorts of cool jobs. Of course they help you bite and chew up food, but they also help you talk. Try this:

🦷 Open your mouth as wide as you can and try to make a *t* sound. Good luck.

🦷 Now close your mouth, clench your teeth, and try to make a *th* sound.

🦷 Open wide again and try to make an *s* sound. Try a *j* while you're at it too.

Aren't you glad your teeth and the rest of your mouth work together so nicely to help you talk? It's like a team in your mouth. God knew exactly what He was doing.

RICH ANSWERS YOUR QUESTIONS
(WHETHER YOU ASKED THEM OR NOT)

It's time again to deal with some pressing questions you did not ask. The topic is **HUMAN HAIR**.

Q: Does our hair have a life span?

A: Yes, hair lasts between one and six years, and then it falls off. See ya. The average person loses one hundred hairs each day. Fortunately, you continue making more all the time (until you start going bald, that is).

Q: On average, how many hairs does a person have on their head?

A: The average number is one hundred thousand.

Q: How fast does hair grow?

A: On average, hair grows about a half inch per month. That works out to be about six inches per year. If you multiply that times the one hundred thousand hairs on your head, that means you grow about nine miles of hair each year!

Hairy Bonus Activity:
Depending on the color of your hair, you may have more or less hair than people with other colors of hair. Draw lines to match the hair colors with the average number of hairs you think a person with that color of hair possesses. Check page 128 for the answers.

90,000 — Black hair

110,000 — Red hair

140,000 — Blond hair

BRAIN EXERCISE

Everyone knows that our bodies need exercise to stay in good shape. Do our brains need exercise too? Sure they do! Here are a few brainteasers to keep your brain in tip-top shape.

1. I am used to bat with, yet I never get a hit. I am near a ball, yet it is never thrown. What am I?

2. A news program brings a special guest onto the show, an archaeologist. The host pulls out a coin that he claims is one of the most amazing finds in recent history. On one side there's an engraving of Caesar, while on the other side the date 63 B.C. appears. Immediately the archaeologist declares the coin a fraud. Why?

3. I never was, but will always be. As soon as I arrive, then I am gone. Everyone depends on me, but they don't always look forward to me. What am I?

Check page 128 for the answers.

IT'S SIMPLE—IT'S A PIMPLE!

It's time for your favorite segment featuring something gross. After all, not everything in the world can be cute and cuddly, so now we're going to talk about pimples.

For most people pimples are a normal part of growing up. There's nothing wrong with you if you get pimples. In fact, about 80 percent of you will have to deal with pimples eventually—so let's "face" the problem. (Get it?)

The trouble starts when you hit puberty and your body starts going through some changes. Certain glands in your skin start making sebum, a gunky fat that is supposed to help your skin stay stretchy and soft. Unfortunately, sometimes the sebum gets trapped in a pore (a tiny hole in your skin), along with dead skin cells and bacteria, and it all starts collecting under your skin. Before you know it, there's a volcano on the tip of your nose waiting to blow.

Now what? You have some choices. You can panic, but stress can make matters worse, so skip that option. Most people will feel the urge to squeeze the pimple. Don't do that! In case you missed that last sentence because it was so short, I'll repeat it for you. *Don't do that!* Squeezing the pimple is the worst thing you could do. When you squeeze it, you risk spreading bacteria and making everything worse. Plus you can permanently scar your face.

The best option is to keep your face clean and just ride it out. Gently cleanse your face a couple of times a day with a mild soap or cleanser. If all else fails, there are medications available to help with the problem.

Oh, one last thing: Be Christlike and don't tease someone who is dealing with pimples. That can *really* leave lasting scars.

DROP-DEAD GORGEOUS

God created you in His image. If you stop to think about it, that's pretty amazing. Nothing else in the world is as special to God as human beings.

Sometimes people are unhappy with the way they look. This makes God sad because what matters is our character. Yes, it's important to take care of the body God has given us, but sometimes we worry too much about external appearances. People spend millions of dollars on cosmetic surgeries because they feel unhappy about how they look.

Botulinum toxin is beyond a doubt the deadliest known protein in the world. Two pounds of it would be enough to kill everyone on the planet. Doesn't this sound like something you would want to stay away from? Yet each year millions of people inject some of this protein into their face to treat wrinkles. Maybe you've heard the product's name before: Botox.

A few people die when that toxin spreads beyond the injection site. It saddens me that people are willing to risk their lives because they're unhappy about the way they look.

Remember, no one is more valuable to God than anyone else. God loves you just the way you are.

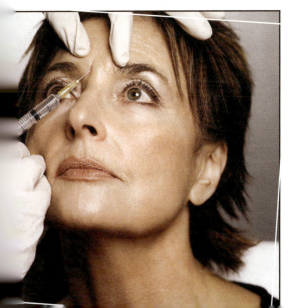

"I praise you because I am fearfully and wonderfully made; your works are wonderful, I know that full well" (Psalm 139:14).

PRETTY UGLY

You may have heard the expression *that's pretty ugly*. It's odd that *pretty* and *ugly* would be used together when they are basically opposites. This is called an oxymoron.

Oxymorons aside, who decides what's pretty and what's ugly? Who decides what's scary and what's not so scary? Unfortunately, we live in a world dominated by a pop culture that tells many people how to think and what do to, what's beautiful and what's not. Sadly, many people follow pop culture's suggestions without thinking.

If you are holding this book, I am talking to you. I want you to understand that external beauty is about a millimeter thick. The beauty that counts is on the inside, so don't ever let anyone around you, on TV, or in a book ever put you down or convince you that they're somehow better than you. As a matter of fact, if they are saying that, they're proving my point: on the inside, where it counts, they are actually quite ugly.

Your goal: take care of your outside and inside, but be beautiful on the inside. Everyone I've ever met that has God on the inside is an amazingly beautiful person!

HELP YOURSELF

Unfortunately, we aren't born with an instruction booklet. The Bible gives us some guidelines, but we can learn even more about how to take care of our bodies. Good health makes a person happier, and I'm sure God wants you to be healthy and happy!

Fortunately, there are many scientists out there trying to learn what makes our bodies function best. Here are several tips to get you started on your way to a healthier you!

AVOID A SUPER-HEAVY BACKPACK
Backpacks are a great way to carry all your school stuff, but if you don't use it right it could hurt you. Don't overload it, and always wear it on both shoulders.

DON'T EAT RED MEAT
We've all heard that red meat is bad, but is it true? A twenty-eight-year study of one hundred thousand people showed that eating red meat will give you a 13 percent higher risk of dying prematurely. Wow! One out of every eight people will die early because they ate red meat regularly.

CURB YOUR SODA INTAKE
"But I love soda!" you say. Of course you do. A little bit of soda once in a while is one thing, but many people drink a ton of the stuff every day without realizing how bad it is for the body. Both diet and regular soft drinks are destroying people, and there are dozens of studies to prove it. So go easy on the soda.

GET OUT OF THAT CHAIR!
Yes, I know that video game you're playing is cool, but you need to also make time to move more than just your fingers—get up and go outside! Play sports and move all your muscle groups, breathe fresh air, and get the blood flowing.

SUMMER OLYMPICS!

Do you get just as excited as I do about the Summer Olympics? Every four years some of the best athletes in the world join to compete in twenty-six sports and hundreds of events. Of course, it's too much to watch all the events, but it's fun to watch a few. In my home the swimming events are the favorites.

Since I love all things nature, I'm drawn to the events that involve as much nature as possible. Many of the events, such as swimming and rowing, wouldn't be possible without water, which God created. Marathons, golfing, and kayaking take place in wonderful outdoor locations. Some sports, such as weight lifting and cycling, require amazing physical preparation.

The majority of Olympic athletes work hard to keep their bodies in great shape. Since God created us, it's pretty obvious we're supposed to be respectful of our bodies. There are many verses in the Bible that talk about caring for our bodies. Not only does that mean paying attention to the things we put into them, it also means staying in good shape by exercising.

What about piercing your body? Or

OLYMPIC QUIZ
Which one of these was an actual Olympic event at one time

☐ Capture the flag
☐ Tug-of-war
☐ Three-legged race

getting a tattoo? We all know that piercing your body means making cuts or holes in it. Tattooing involves damaging your skin with a needle and injecting it with ink to get your immune system to engulf the ink and your skin to permanently heal over it. Neither of these seems to be a great way of glorifying God with our bodies.

AN OLYMPICS-WORTHY MOTTO
"So whether you eat or drink or whatever you do, do it all for the glory of God" (1 Corinthians 10:31).

Athletes competing in the Olympics this summer are pretty serious about keeping their bodies in the best shape. I hope you will also be serious about taking care of the body God gave you!

A TERRIBLE SPORT
In the 1900 Olympics (and fortunately only in the 1900 Olympics) there was an event called live pigeon shooting. Pigeons were released, and the participants had to shoot as many birds as possible from the sky! How awful. I'm glad this messy and bloody event was stopped immediately.

117

DO YOU HEAR WHAT I HEAR?

Sound is measured in hertz (Hz), which indicates the frequency of the sound wave. Humans can typically hear sounds between twenty and twenty thousand hertz. Sounds below twenty hertz are called infrasound waves. They are made by avalanches, whales, and earthquakes. Sounds above twenty thousand hertz are called ultrasound waves and can be heard by a large variety of creatures.

We've all been told that dogs can hear high pitches that we can't hear. Actually, their range of hearing goes more than twice as high as ours! But that's nothing compared to these other awesome hearers:

HUMAN:	Between 20 Hz and 20,000 Hz
DOG:	Between 67 Hz and 45,000 Hz
BAT:	Between 20 Hz and 120,000 Hz
ATLANTIC BOTTLENOSE DOLPHIN:	Between 75 Hz and 150,000 Hz
NOCTUID MOTH:	Between 1,000 Hz and 240,000 Hz

It's the same with light. For example, the LED light on the front of your TV remote control puts out infrared light. Humans can't see it, but we know it's there because we see its effects. It's the same with God: we may not see or hear Him, but we see the effects of God in our lives when we make Him number one.

TRY THIS!

Most digital cameras can see infrared light, so if you look at the LED on your remote control with a digital camera, you should be able to see the light it produces when you push a button on the remote.

SPEAKING OF LANGUAGES

We speak both English and Spanish in our home. I lived in France for a year and learned a bit of French too. Researchers believe there are between six thousand and seven thousand languages spoken in the world today. Some estimates are even higher. Wow, that's a lot of different languages! Of course, the Bible says the division of languages started at the Tower of Babel.

The honeybee was created in a unique way because you could say that it has its own language too. It does something called the waggle dance.

When a honeybee finds food, it comes back to the hive and does a figure-eight movement that tells the other bees exactly where they can find a new source of food. By the time the dance is done, other bees can exit the hive and know which direction to travel and how far they need to go! It's amazing how God included the most amazing little details in each of His creatures.

你好 नमस्ते Hello

The top three languages in the world
(those with the most native speakers) are:
1. MANDARIN CHINESE 2. HINDI 3. ENGLISH

YOUR BUILT-IN INSTRUMENT

I never cease to be amazed by the bodies God made for us. God thought of everything.

I want to talk about your voice box or larynx. It's an organ in your neck that is about two inches long, and it enables you to talk and make sounds. The voice box is also involved in breathing and helps protect you from getting food or water into your lungs.

The sounds are made when your lungs pump air up through your voice box. Your vocal chords come together and vibrate as air passes through them. (Try holding your breath and talking. Yeah, it's not going to work.) Your mouth does the last step by shaping those sounds into words using your tongue, teeth, palate (roof of your mouth), lips, and so on. It's quite an amazing sequence of actions that have to occur in order for you to talk!

Still none of this is worth anything if your brain can't first command all these steps to happen and decide what words your mouth needs to say. That is ultimately the most important part. And now the big question: What is coming out of your mouth? Good stuff? Bad stuff? Your mouth has the ability to cause incredible damage to the people around you as well as to yourself.

Here's a good rule: Never use your mouth to tear people down; use it only to build people up.

HOW MUCH CONTROL DO YOU HAVE OF YOUR TONGUE? CAN YOU—

- Roll your tongue into a U-shaped tube?
- Pull your tongue down and fold it backward?
- Flip your tongue upside down?
- Touch your nose with your tongue?

SCRATCH THE ITCH

It's no secret that our bodies have a lot of amazing functions. It's also not a secret that some of the things they do seem pretty odd or even gross. Fear not—that is why I write this "Yuck!" page, to remind you that even things that appear gross can also show us how much detail went into the design of our bodies.

Here's something that everyone has to deal with: itching. The moment I typed the word *itching,* I had to scratch my head. Isn't that odd? How about you? Now that I mentioned itching, do you suddenly have an itch somewhere?

The average human body is covered with about twenty square feet of skin. That's like the top of one of those big six-foot folding tables at church. Every single day of your life, your skin touches stuff, so there's really no way to avoid getting an itch here and there.

Your basic itch occurs when your skin comes in contact with things such as bugs, dust, clothing, and hair. A serious itch can be caused by allergies, disease, infections, and even emotions. Much like your response to tickling, itching is a built-in defense mechanism that tells your body something bad might be going on. Your skin sends a signal to your brain, and, voilà, your brain tells your hand to come to the rescue. Scratch, scratch, *ahhhhh*.

YOU'VE GOT NERVE

As many of you know, *Guide* magazine has a very cool Web site with many neat things to do and read. It's also a place where you can post comments or ask me questions. Recently a reader asked if I could write about the nervous system.

Most of you have electrical outlets and lights all over the walls and ceilings of your home. Behind the walls, wires connect all those items to one main electrical panel. The nervous system in your body is similar; it's basically your body's electrical wiring system.

Your nervous system is made of nerves that start in the brain and central spinal cord and branch out to every other part of your body, sending little messages.

Neurons send these signals through your body at amazing speeds and help all your body parts work together, making sure they're all doing what they're supposed to do. Your brain, considered by many to be the most complex organism in the universe, is at the center of the action, connected by about one hundred million neurons.

To believe that this could have randomly evolved from nothing is perhaps one of the enemy's biggest hoaxes. The Bible teaches that we were carefully designed by God.

SUPER FOOD AND RICH'S MUDDY QUINOA

As you know, I love to talk about nature. I rarely talk about food, though, and food is edible nature! Because I'm a vegetarian, all the food I eat comes from plants.

One of my newest favorite foods is quinoa (pronounced like "keen-wah"). Over the past few years this grain, grown mainly in South America, has become more and more popular in North America. It's even been called a "super food"!

When I hear the term *super food*, I tend to think of a banana with a cape flying through the air, but that's not what's meant. A super food is a food that has high nutritional value. Quinoa is high in fiber, protein, and other important nutrients, and it even has calcium! Some people think you can get calcium only from dairy products, but plant foods with calcium are dark, leafy green veggies such as kale, collard greens, broccoli, and also nuts and seeds.

So how do you eat quinoa? Since I love to cook and invent my own recipes, I'm going to include one of my favorite easy-to-make quinoa recipes. Maybe you'll enjoy this super-delicious super food as much as I do!

RICH'S MUDDY QUINOA

Ingredients:
- 1 cup quinoa, cooked and cooled
- 1 can black beans, drained and rinsed
- 1/2 cup green pepper, chopped
- 1/2 cup cilantro, chopped
- 1/2 cup green onions, chopped

Instructions:
Mix all ingredients together. Dress to taste with olive oil, lemon juice, and salt.

A GROSS CELEBRATION

I'd like to dedicate these next two pages to some of my favorite gross things. You may think it's strange to call them my favorite gross things, but even if they're gross, they're a part of our wonderful, living bodies that God created. We should try to appreciate even the little gross details!

Snot
It's not glamorous, but it is one of our normal body fluids. As air moves back and forth through your nose, your snot, I mean, your mucous membrane, is like a sticky doormat that stops germs and dust from getting any farther into your body. Our bodies can make almost a quart of mucus each day. Snot bad, huh?

Eye gunk
That's not what it's officially called, but that has got to be the best name for it. We all get it in the morning, but we're not sure why. It's actually a type of mucus that keeps the moisture in your eyes from evaporating. During the day you blink, and the mucus gets moved around, but at night when your eyes are closed, it has nowhere to go, so a little leaks out the sides of your eyelids.

Urine

OK, yes, I'm talking about you-know-what. No one likes to talk about it, but it is a natural part of our bodily functions. The shocking thing about urine is that it is a sterile body fluid! That means it's cleaner than your hands after you've washed them. In the old days, urine, which is rich in ammonia, was used as a cleaning fluid. In ancient Rome it was used for whitening teeth. Now *that* is gross!

Burping

When we were babies, our moms and dads had to pat us on our backs after we drank milk so that we would burp. Ah, how cute! But now that you're bigger, if you burp at the table you might find yourself on your way to your room. Burping happens when you get air in your stomach. Your digestive system doesn't want air in there, so your body tries to squeeze it back out through your esophagus. *Burp.* Oops—excuse me.

Dandruff

I like snow, but not when it's made of clumps of oily dead skin falling off my head. That's dandruff. Every day your skin sheds dead skin cells. Most of the dust floating around in your house is made of dead skin cells. The skin on your head also produces oil. When you mix dead skin cells and oil, they

stick together, and you end up with clumps of oily dead skin on your head. When you have too much of that action going on, it may look like there's a snowstorm swirling around you.

WHO NOSE WHAT THAT SMELL IS?

Sniff, sniff. What's that smell?

The sense of smell is amazing. For example, it can help you identify certain things. Has the milk gone bad? Ask your nose. Is there a fire? Ask your nose. Is it time for a shower after playing sports all day? Don't bother asking your nose—just go take a shower.

Olfaction, the fancy word for "sense of smell," is a neat thing that God built into our body's design. It's the way our body recognizes certain chemical molecules in the air. Our brains analyze the information and then tells us what we're smelling.

As for those molecules, they're incredibly tiny—so tiny that they're measured in nanometers. And just how big is a nanometer? Check out the measuring stick. See the tiny millimeter lines? Well, each millimeter equals one million nanometers!

But back to your nose. Imagine your mom or dad is making a fresh batch of cookies. (*Mmm!*) Odor molecules are released from the cookies as they bake. These molecules are smaller than one nanometer, and they float through the air, since gravity doesn't have much of an effect on them. When you inhale those molecules, your nose's receptors detect the odor molecules and tell your brain to identify them. In this case, they send out an urgent message: cookies!

TRY THIS AT HOME!

We can taste only four things: sweet, sour, salt, and bitter. It's the odors we can smell with our nose that makes each flavor unique.

Try this simple experiment at home with a friend. Have your friend wear a blindfold and then feed him or her small pieces of different foods. Now, add this twist: Hold (secretly or not) a different piece of food under their nose while they try to guess what they're eating. What happens?

It seems weird, but we do most of our tasting with our nose!

WARNING: COLD SEASON AHEAD!

A lot of people will catch a cold this winter, even if they live in a warm place. That's because colds are caused by a virus that spreads. Here are a few things you can do to help avoid getting a cold this winter:

- Wash your hands often.
- Keep your hands away from your eyes, nose, and mouth.
- Avoid people who are coughing and sneezing.
- Get enough sleep to keep your immune system strong.
- Eat healthy food and get adequate exercise.
- Drink plenty of fluids.

ANSWER KEY

p. 43 Baby Animal Names: **porcupine**, porcupette; **turtle**, hatchling; **cockroach**, nymph; **goose**, gosling; **turkey**, poult; **ant**, antling; **oyster**, spat; **cheetah**, cub; **ferret**, kit; **swan**, cygnet; **platypus**, puggle; **kangaroo**, joey; **goat**, kid; **camel**, calf; **peacock**, peachick; **owl**, owlet; **fly**, maggot; **bee**, larva

p. 102 The Tongue: salty, sour, sweet, savory, bitter

p. 107 Eye Test: Mud!

p. 110 Human Hair: 90,000, red; 110,000, black; 140,000, blonde

p. 111 Brain Exercise: 1. eyelashes 2. B.C. stands for "before Christ." This dating system wasn't used till after Christ had been born. 3. tomorrow

p. 117 Olympic Quiz: tug-of-war

GOT A QUESTION FOR RICH?
Ask your toughest nature and science questions at
www.guidemagazine.org/mud.